BEDEVILED

Lewis, Tolkien and
the Shadow of Evil

COLIN DURIEZ

IVP Books

An imprint of InterVarsity Press
Downers Grove, Illinois

InterVarsity Press
P.O. Box 1400, Downers Grove, IL 60515-1426
ivpress.com
email@ivpress.com

InterVarsity Press® is the book-publishing division of InterVarsity Christian Fellowship/USA®, a movement of students and faculty active on campus at hundreds of universities, colleges and schools of nursing in the United States of America, and a member movement of the International Fellowship of Evangelical Students. For information about local and regional activities, visit intervarsity.org.

Scripture quotations, unless otherwise noted, are from The Holy Bible, English Standard Version, copyright © 2001 by Crossway Bibles, a division of Good News Publishers. Used by permission. All rights reserved.

Cover design: Cindy Kiple
Interior design: Beth McGill
Images: old typewriter: © slobo/iStockphoto
   WWII battle scene: © Johncairns/iStockphoto
   blank key from manual typewriter: © FlamingPumkin/iStockphoto

ISBN 978-0-8308-3417-4 (print)
ISBN 978-0-8308-9812-1 (digital)

Printed in the United States of America ∞

Library of Congress Cataloging-in-Publication Data
A catalog record for this book is available from the Library of Congress.

P 20 19 18 17 16 15 14 13 12 11 10 9 8 7 6 5 4 3 2 1

Y 32 31 30 29 28 27 26 25 24 23 22 21 20 19 18 17 16 15

To Ian Blakemore

Contents

Hobgoblin nor foul fiend
Can daunt his spirit,
He knows he at the end
Shall life inherit.

THE PILGRIM SONG,
JOHN BUNYAN

Introduction

There are dangers in talking about a cosmic battle between good and evil. Most of all, it implies for many people that a permanent battle is raging between the forces of darkness and light. This is far from the understanding of C. S. Lewis and his friends in the now famous Oxford literary group, the Inklings. They mainly saw a figure such as the devil not as equal with God but as a created spiritual being of some kind, an angel of high rank, who had turned deliberately to evil from his original goodness. Though we are used to thinking of the universe very much in material, physical terms, the friends believed—and Lewis was in the vanguard of arguing for—a larger view of reality, a supernatural one.

Nevertheless, it was clear to them that a battle between good and evil was in process, both in the unseen world and in the physical and psychological horrors of human warfare. Most of the core members of the Inklings had experienced battle in World War I. Some bore physical or mental scars. Were they alive today, their view of a spiritual conflict behind physical battles, which affected whether or not people could live at peace and free from terror, would undoubtedly be reinforced. J. R. R. Tolkien for instance considered that the weapons of Sauron, the Dark Lord of *The Lord of the Rings*, had been used by the allies as well as the enemy in World

War II, and C. S. Lewis expressed grave doubts about the massive bombings of civilians.

Because, among the Inklings, Lewis was at the forefront of writing on human pain, suffering, devilry, miracles and the supernatural, he provides the main focus of this book. This is not to say that other Inklings members did not write extensively on these themes—most famously, Tolkien in his *The Lord of the Rings*. They therefore come into my book, where relevant, as much as possible in its short compass. The chronology of Lewis's writings is followed to a large extent in part two. In part one, his writings are more tied into his experience of two world wars, even though the more recent war was not a firsthand one for him. In part one, we also look at Tolkien's *The Lord of the Rings*, in its relevance to the imagery of war and evil. Tolkien's story, of course, is well known throughout the globe in its original print form, and now through Peter Jackson's blockbuster movie version.

It is worth pointing out from the onset that C. S. Lewis had no interest in writing literally about what goes on in the afterlife to satisfy curiosity about this. He doesn't take up popular imagery that is supposedly describing what happens when the spirit leaves the body at death, imagery that might portray a tunnel with light in the distance (based on accounts of near-death experiences). His accounts of heaven and hell are very different from each other according to the purpose of the book: there are different sets of imagery in his dream story, *The Great Divorce*, which is about an excursion by bus from hell to the borderlands of heaven, and the Narnian story *The Last Battle*. *The Screwtape Letters* is cast in yet another pattern of imagery, in which hell resembles a mixture of rampant bureaucracy like in Hitler's Third Reich and a ruthless modern corporation. His treatment of the afterlife and the supernatural world is therefore in stark contrast to Richard Matheson's bestselling novel *What Dreams May Come* (also made into a movie), which claims to be based on research and to give factual details of heaven and hell. In his brief prologue to his reader, Richard Matheson says, "Because [the novel's] subject is survival after death, it is essential that you realize, before reading the story, that only one aspect of it is fictional: the characters and their relationships." He adds, "With few exceptions, every other detail is derived exclusively from research."[1] He even provides a bibliography, including titles that are based on theosophy, a movement which seeks hidden knowledge for enlightenment and salvation.

Lewis was careful to state the opposite. Where he writes fictionally about the unseen world, and heaven and hell, he is not writing factually and literally about the afterlife. He warned in his preface to *The Great Divorce*:

> I beg readers to remember that this is a fantasy. It has of course—or I intended it to have—a moral. But the transmortal conditions are solely an imaginative supposal: they are not even a guess or a speculation at what may actually await us. The last thing I wish is to arouse factual curiosity about the details of the after-world.[2]

In his youth he had dabbled in the occult (ironically, this was in his long period as an atheist) and realized the dangers of its compulsive attraction for him. Though he firmly believed in the actuality of heaven and hell, in his fictional books he explored these realities through what he called "supposals" in stories of his own making—though these did draw upon the imaginations of other writers such John Milton, Dante and many others from his extensive reading. He also regarded biblical imagery of heaven and hell as authority of the first order. In *The Problem of Pain* and elsewhere he offered logical arguments defending the reality of heaven, hell and immortality, based on Christian doctrines as embodied in the historic church creeds.

C. S. Lewis could root our human struggles with good and bad in our ordinary lives now, because for him heaven and hell were best understood in relation to them. He had a central Christian worldview in which heaven, in the final analysis, is really the world as it was meant to be, and is now the future condition of the world, which is in process of being radically remade. Lewis once wrote, "To enter heaven is to become more human than you ever succeeded in being in earth; to enter hell, is to be banished from humanity."[3] This process began in the death and resurrection of Christ, which inaugurated the new creation. Hell is conversely the world stripped of meaning, twisted and despoiled beyond recognition. Compared with the reality of heaven, it is almost nothing (as Lewis brilliantly pictures in his *The Great Divorce*). One of the Inklings, Charles Williams, was fond of saying, "Hell is always inaccurate." Places like Auschwitz or starving towns under siege in Syria's civil war as I write are modern hints of what hell is like, real nightmare images of unutterable loss created by modern human wickedness. For C. S. Lewis, and for friends like Tolkien and Charles Williams, there are intelligent powers pitted against goodness that are bent on destroying or breaking what is good, such as our very humanity. This is why we get glimpses of hell starkly in places like Auschwitz or in acts like genocide, but also (as Lewis constantly reminds us) on an ordinary level in deliberately wrong choices we make that have far-reaching and escalating consequences for ourselves and others, very often those we love.

In the concern of Lewis and friends with the powers of good and evil, I suggest, lies a key to their global popularity and continued relevance in particular in the new millennium. They bring these powers home to us. Lewis applied traditional Christian teaching about the world, the flesh and the devil to modern, often subtle manifestations of evil. He did this with such freshness and imagination that readers of his fiction are often unaware of the presence of orthodox Christian teaching. Numerous readers who do not share Lewis's faith have long enjoyed *The Screwtape Letters*, the most famous of his books on devilry, because of its uncanny realism about human foibles. The popularity of the book owes much to the unlikely but brilliantly successful combination of humor with exploring the serious subject of human damnation.

As well as particularly modern manifestations of evil such as global war, Lewis was concerned with the perennial problem of what he called "worldliness," where we focus on this world alone, losing its context in the infinite vistas of the unseen, supernatural world. The limited perspective of worldliness is explored rigorously in *The Screwtape Letters*. The fact that other major figures of his literary circle of friends, such as Charles Williams and J. R. R. Tolkien, were also preoccupied with the lure of the dark side and the spell it casts gave Lewis moral support and encouragement as he explored difficult issues like devilry and human suffering.

An ancient meaning of *spell* in English is "story." Lewis, like Tolkien and other friends, was casting a spell in telling his stories of temptation, the powers of good and evil, and ways out of entrapment to badness. During World War II he said,

> Spells are used for breaking enchantments as well as for inducing them. And you and I have need of the strongest spell that can be found to wake us from the enchantment of worldliness. . . . Almost our whole education has been directed to silencing this shy, persistent, inner voice; almost all our philosophies have been devised to convince us that the good man is to be found on this earth.[4]

I mentioned that other major figures of his literary circle, the Inklings, such as Williams and Tolkien, were also preoccupied with the demonic and the associated problem of evil. Sauron, the lieutenant of Tolkien's Satan, Melkor, dominates the plot of *The Lord of the Rings*, much of it being read as it was written to the Inklings. (Tolkien in fact dedicated the first edition to the group.) Charles Williams wrote several nonfictional and fictional works on a similar theme, including a historical study of witchcraft and his novel *All Hallows Eve*, which benefited from input from the Inklings. Lewis's science-fiction stories *Perelandra* and *That Hideous Strength* (particularly the latter) were influenced by Williams and were among several of Lewis's writings, including *The Great Divorce*, on a devilish or a related purgatorial theme. Tolkien's short story "Leaf by Niggle" reflects the interest that the Inklings had in the topic of purgatory in the World War II years—perhaps their most important period.

The concerns with devilry and related issues like human suffering are also there in writings between the wars and after World War II, but the last war gave intensity to them. Such writings before and after the war include C. S. Lewis's *The Pilgrim's Regress* (Lewis's first work of fiction, which we shall explore in chap. 7) and the Narnian stories *The Lion, the Witch and the Wardrobe*, *Prince Caspian* and *The Last Battle* (see chap. 9). Writings from others include Charles Williams's *Descent into Hell* (written before he became a member of the Inklings), and even Tolkien's *The Hobbit*, with the terrifying dragon Smaug, the goblin-ridden mountains and the Battle of the Five Armies.

Some chapters of this book fill out the context of the concern of Lewis and his friends with devilry. The times they lived through helped to draw attention to the urgency of such themes, which could be decidedly unpleasant to write about (as Lewis found when writing *The Screwtape Letters*). The emotional and physical scars of World War I were reopened when the Inklings found themselves living through a second global conflict just over two decades later. Between the two modern wars, Lewis went through the dramatic changes of his movement from atheism to Christian belief. I have briefly portrayed some of the remarkable contrasts and similarities between the younger and older Lewis, as well as the concerns of the group of

Lewis's friends in the productive World War II years. This has meant focusing on the emergence of devilry and related themes of the human quest for heaven or descent into hell, and the search for a way out of the self. I also occasionally consider writings of Dorothy L. Sayers, a mutual friend of Lewis and Charles Williams, where particularly relevant. Ms. Sayers was famous for her crime stories featuring Lord Peter Wimsey, plays, broadcasts, translations and popular theology. Because of an important link C. S. Lewis forges between the concerns of the Inklings and those of Sayers, it is difficult to ignore her work when considering the "life-force" of the Inklings.[5]

The Screwtape Letters, more than any other book by a member of the Inklings, draws dramatic attention to the theme of devilry in their writings. How it began in Lewis's mind gives a unique insight into the link between the lives of the Inklings and their writings that carried the theme of the very real powers of light and darkness.

part
one

Understanding Evil During a Time of War

1

C. S. Lewis in Wartime

The Cosmic Battle

World War II had been running its course for less than a year. Wartime had brought many changes into C. S. Lewis's life, but he valued the normality of attending his local Anglican church. On the Sunday morning of July 21, 1940, he left his home, The Kilns, briskly as usual, for nearby Headington Quarry and Holy Trinity Church. As he walked, the familiar wooded slopes of Shotover Hill were behind him, and he enjoyed the rural quiet. There was the occasional sound of traffic from the main road nearby, inevitable even early on Sunday so close to Oxford.

Just the Friday evening before, Lewis's family doctor, "Humphrey" Havard, had driven up to The Kilns. It was not a medical visit to see him, Mrs. Moore, Maureen her daughter, or one of the evacuee children billeted with them. Havard was also one of his friends from the Inklings. As planned, they tuned in and listened on the radio to a speech by Hitler. The BBC provided a simultaneous translation. A possible answer to a puzzle occurred to Lewis as he listened—how was the German leader so convincing to so many? Though Lewis rarely read the daily newspapers, he of course knew Hitler's claims were grossly untrue. Making what he blatantly called his "final appeal to common sense," Hitler boasted, "It never has been my intention to wage war, but rather to build up a State with a new social order and the finest possible standard of culture."[1]

Hitler's emotive speech may have still tugged at Lewis's mind in the quietness of his church that Sunday. England faced the very real danger of invasion by Hitler's forces, driven and maintained like a machine. The Battle of Britain, one of the deciding battles of the war, had begun—just that very day, nearly two hundred patrols were sent up into the summer skies by the Royal Air Force in response to enemy aircraft threatening Britain. During the church liturgy and bad hymns (as Lewis regarded them) he found his thoughts turning to the master of evil, Satan. Somehow, the arrogant dictator resembled him—not least in the size of his ego and self-centeredness. In the jumble of thoughts jostling with words of a great tradition, it struck Lewis that a war-orientated bureaucracy was a more appropriate image of hell for people ignorant of the past than a traditional one. Here was Hitler bent on taking over and ruling European countries, including England. There was the devil, who had designs to exert his will systematically over all parts of human life, his ultimate aim being dehumanization—the "abolition of man," as Lewis later called it.

Lewis's brother Warren ("Warnie") had been evacuated just a few weeks previously. This was just before many thousands of re-treating British soldiers were snatched from the beaches and jetties of the nearest French port of Dunkirk by ships and by boats large and small. Warnie, a retired army major, had been called back the previous year into military service and dispatched to France, which had been partly occupied by German forces. That quiet Sunday afternoon Lewis told Warnie in a letter an idea that would ger-minate and grow, and eventually become *The Screwtape Letters*. The idea was for a book containing the correspondence between a senior and a junior devil. It resulted in an important figure in hell's "Lowerarchy" (Screwtape, the senior devil) writing convincingly to

Wormwood (the junior devil, Screwtape's nephew) about devilish ways of winning over human beings or keeping them safe in the clutches of his "Father Below." Screwtape in fact would expertly model himself upon his master, the "father of lies," also known as "Our Father Below."

As the book idea developed, C. S. Lewis made the connection between the traditional conflict of good and evil and the imagery of modern warfare, with its terror, apocalyptic weapons and global reach. Lewis had lived through World War I and experienced trench warfare on its front line in France. Some of Lewis's most popular writings on the forces of evil and goodness came into existence in the second global war, with its even more advanced modern weapons of terror.

As Hitler's broadcast made clear, his story of the racial superiority and heroic destiny of his particular nation was compelling to millions of ordinary, contemporary people, despite being a vicious cocktail of lies. While he was listening to it, Lewis felt himself being drawn into its devilish spell. He confessed to Warnie in that letter, which he started writing on the day after the broadcast, "I don't know if I'm weaker than other people but it is a positive revelation to me how *while the speech lasts* it is impossible not to waver just a little. I should be useless as a schoolmaster or a policeman."[2]

Lewis evidently pondered how Hitler's deceptive story, with its carefully crafted plausibility, revealed new things about the ancient nature of evil. The egotistical and self-absorbed leader of Germany fitted well into his own theory of "chronological snobbery." Lewis had been disillusioned with this attitude in the 1920s through the influence of his friend Owen Barfield. Chronological snobbery was his name given to the all-pervasive belief that the modern view of x is inevitably superior to past ways of seeing x. Older views, to the modern, simply had been left behind by progress.

Then there was the larger vista of war itself, made even more ghastly in its modern forms, such as the present war. World War I had been renamed from "The Great War" because of its total reach. The new war (at that time Lewis called it "the European war") had already dramatically reached in its destruction and desolation more deeply into cities. The new scale of the bombing of civilians made the attacks by zeppelins in World War I tiny in comparison. Lewis's thoughts at this time are not recorded, but their outcome in *The Screwtape Letters* suggest ruminations along these lines in his imagery of hell as a mix of bureaucracy and techniques that might be found in a ruthlessly pragmatic modern business. Tolkien's own similar thoughts, recorded in letters, reveal concerns about the triumph of machinery as a devilish power ("the weapons of Sauron") in World War II. As the Screwtape idea increasingly took flight, Lewis shows evidence of thinking about what modern warfare revealed about the age-old battle for the human soul. In Lewis's humble church in Headington Quarry, in a tranquil Oxford suburb, the talk often was, as it had been for centuries, of a cosmic battle against the world, the flesh and the devil.[3] This tradition of such talk had a powerful reality for Lewis as he responded by standing, sitting and kneeling during the liturgy of that July morning service of Holy Communion, a service as familiar to him as his old slippers waiting for him at home.

The years when Lewis lived through World War I and then World War II provide startling insight into his preoccupation with devilry—the powers of evil—and goodness. His differing experience of the global wars, both unprecedented in history before the twentieth century, represent a quest and a growth in Lewis as thinker, writer and storyteller—and as a person. It now seems natural to us for a book like *The Screwtape Letters* to be begotten during a war that is to us a typically modern, all-out conflict. Many wars now seem to be, in words now common to brave journalists at the scene, "of biblical proportions" or "apocalyptic." What remains surprising, indeed remarkable, is that Lewis, seemingly without effort, could approach his subject with humor and biting satire, without alienating his readers even today by diminishing the horror of evil and human suffering.

We therefore need initially to explore the context of Lewis's pre-occupation with devilry in the two global, technologically advanced wars that touched his life irrevocably—both conflicts never before suffered by so many people at once in human history and both revealingly characteristic of our era (an era Lewis was to call the "Age of the Machine").

The Shadow of War

C. S. Lewis, or "Jack," as friends and family knew him, was only fifteen when World War I began in August 1914 and the world changed forever. He was to reach the trenches of northern France around his nineteenth birthday. During this period of adolescence he was a convinced atheist of sorts, tending at first to be a rather solitary, self-contained person.[4] He had no mother, having lost her to cancer before he was ten. Mainly he confided in his brother, Warnie, two years his elder, but saw little of him during these years due first to the separation of schooling and then to Warnie's service with the British army. He, like his brother, found it difficult if not impossible to find an affinity with his father. He did however find a soulmate in Arthur Greeves, a boy three years his senior who lived very near him on an opulent fringe of Belfast. Lewis corresponded with Arthur throughout the World War I years and, indeed, until his death in 1963, the letters providing insight into Lewis's life, development and particularly his early thinking. Arthur, a gifted painter, shared a similar taste in reading and all things "northern," such as Old Norse mythology.

C. S. Lewis, privately educated and from a privileged upper-middle-class background, turned eighteen near the end of 1916. The path he saw before him then was one of very basic and brief officer training as part of student life at Oxford University and then being sent into battle. His prospects of survival did not look good. During the First World War one out of every eight men drawn into the conflict from Britain died.[5] Recruits from Oxford and Cambridge Universities, along with others from Britain's social elite, had a very much higher death rate than the average recruit. This is because most became junior officers and led assaults and operations against the enemy, making them particularly vulnerable.[6] The experience of war was to mold his basic ideas about the nature of the universe and inspire a central theme of his writings, which was that of a cosmic war against evil forming a larger context for human battles, whether strife within the individual human soul or bloody conflicts between states.

The "Great Knock"

It was impossible for the young Lewis not to be touched by the conflict, even though he did not train for and then embark for war until 1917, the year before it ended. Most immediately for him, his older brother, Warren, also his friend and confidant, entered the war early on and periodically returned from France on leave. At the beginning of the war Lewis was in the English West Midlands at Malvern College, Worcestershire,[7] and miserable, a state that was to decide his father, Albert, to put him under the tutorage of William T. Kirkpatrick, the "Great Knock." Kirkpatrick, who lived in the village of Bookham, in Surrey, England,[8] was Lewis's tutor from 1914–1917 and nicknamed by him "the Great Knock" because of the impact of his stringent logical mind on the teenager.

Shortly after August 4, 1914, when Germany invaded Belgium and Britain declared war, the British Expeditionary Force landed in France, which Britain had promised to defend. The following month, Lewis began his studies with Kirkpatrick. Near the end of that month, on September 30, Warren, his brother, was commissioned as a second lieutenant in the Royal Army Service Corps. Lewis's rural haven was not unaffected by events. He noted in a letter to

Albert, his father, that "war fever" was raging around the Bookham neighborhood. Soon the village people prepared a cottage for Belgian refugees—with the rapid German push into Belgium tens of thousands of refugees had poured into England.

In early summer 1915 there was the first German zeppelin air attack on nearby London. When the airships bombed Waterloo Railway Station, electric flashes in the skies as a result of the explosions could be seen from Bookham. At least, that was what the locals said it was.[9] This must have brought home to Lewis the reality and threats of modern warfare.

It is clear that Lewis was continually aware of events of war, particularly in France. France for him was not an abstract concept; he and Warren had shared a memorable holiday with their mother, Flora, in 1907 (the year before she died of cancer), in a French coastal town not far from some of the places made familiar by the war. The conflict however failed to erode his deep happiness under the tutorage of Kirkpatrick. For the last part of 1916 Lewis's thoughts and anxieties were focused on passing the entrance exam for Oxford University. For him everything was at stake, as he saw no alternative to an academic career, and it also provided a good entry into officer training, after establishing a future place in an academic career. In December 1916 Lewis accordingly made his first trip to Oxford to take a scholarship examination. This took place between December 5 and 9. Passed over by New College, he received a classical scholarship to University College, Oxford. A few days later the *London Times* newspaper listed among the successful candidates "Clive S. Lewis, University College." By that time, Britain had been at war with Germany for nearly two and a half years.

Oxford

In March 1917, Lewis came into residence at University College, in the Trinity or summer term.[10] This allowed him to start his passage into the army by way of the University Officers' Training Corps. He was officially a student without requirements of formal studies. Despite evidence of the impact of war everywhere Lewis had a pleasant time. He enjoyed the library of the Oxford Union, punting on the River Cherwell or swimming in it. He was very much aware of the general absence of undergraduates in Oxford, and other marks of war in the unusually quiet town. Most of his college building was taken up with serving as an army hospital.

Cadet C. S. Lewis, Keble College

Lewis was assigned a battalion encamped at Keble College, and was able to keep in contact with new acquaintances at University College. It also allowed a life-changing encounter. The alphabet dictated that his roommate was fellow Irishman Edward "Paddy" Moore, a seemingly trivial fact. As an *L*, Lewis was placed in a bare, tiny room with the *M*, Moore. Paddy was the son of Mrs. Janie Moore, who had left an unhappy marriage and Ireland in 1907 to live in Bristol with Paddy and his young sister, Maureen. With Paddy's commission, Mrs. Moore and Maureen moved to Oxford to be near him. She and Lewis first met in June that year, along with others of Paddy's friends. Drawn to the Moore family, Lewis spent more and more time in their company. Maureen, who was eleven at the time, remembered, "Before my brother went out to the trenches in France he asked C. S. Lewis, . . . 'If I don't come back, would you look after my mother and my little sister?'"[11] Mrs. Moore and Maureen were staying in temporary rooms in Wellington Square, not far from Keble College.

Paddy was one of a set of six in their portion of the college. In a letter Lewis described the group as "public school men and varsity [university] men."[12] A look a few months forward to the future reveals the cost of the war. Lewis was to fight with the infantry and to be badly wounded. Paddy Moore was to serve with the 2nd Battalion of the Rifle Brigade, dying at Pargny, France, in March 1918. Martin

Ashworth Somerville was to battle in Egypt and Palestine with the Rifle Brigade, dying in Palestine in September 1918. Alexander Gordon Sutton was to fight with Paddy Moore in the Rifle Brigade and to be killed two months before Paddy. Thomas Kerrison Davy, with the 1st Battalion of the Rifle Brigade, was to be severely wounded near Arras, where Lewis was to fight, in March 1918, dying later. Denis Howard de Pass was to serve with the 12th Battalion of the Rifle Brigade and was reported "wounded and missing" in April 1918. He was given up as dead, but in fact was captured by the enemy, surviving to fight again in World War II.

As the time for active service loomed larger, training became more feverish. Lewis was given a temporary commission in September 1917 as a second lieutenant in the 3rd Battalion, Somerset Light Infantry. Within two months he would be at the front lines in northern France.

After a brief home visit on leave to Belfast, he joined his new regiment at Crownhill, near Plymouth, South Devon. Here he became friends with Laurence Johnson, who had been commissioned just months before him, and like him had been elected to an Oxford College. His new friend was very soon to die in France.[13] Johnson seems to have encouraged him to pursue philosophy.[14] Lewis told Arthur Greeves in a letter that philosophy, particularly metaphysics, was his "great find" at the moment.[15]

To the Front Lines of France

Just under a month after the visit to his father, Lewis suddenly was ordered to go to the front, being allowed only a forty-eight-hour leave. Unable to visit his father again in Ireland within that time, Lewis decided to spend it with Mrs. Moore and Maureen in Bristol, which happened to be on the way back from Plymouth to his departure point for France, desperately telegramming his father to rush to Bristol to see him: "HAVE ARRIVED BRISTOL ON 48 HOURS LEAVE.

REPORT SOUTHAMPTON SATURDAY. CAN YOU COME BRISTOL. IF SO
MEET AT STATION. . . . JACKS." Confused, Albert Lewis simply wired
back: "DON'T UNDERSTAND TELEGRAM. PLEASE WRITE." Thus Lewis
did not see his father again until after he was invalided out of France
the following spring.

Lewis reported to Southampton harbor at 4 p.m. on November
17, 1917, and crossed to France, to a base camp at Monchy-le-Preux,
a place which later inspired one of his war poems, "French Nocturne."[16] By his nineteenth birthday, November 29, Lewis found
himself at the front line and introduced to life in the trenches. His
brother was elsewhere in France and in a safer location.

In mid-December 1917 Lewis was billeted in the French town of
Arras. Though it bore the wounds of three and a half years of war,
it would be disfigured even more the following March, when the
enemy thrust forward in their last major offensive. Lewis and his
colleagues were transported to and from the trenches in buses.[17]
Before Christmas, Lewis was back up in the cold, wet trenches for
a few days, some distance from the main battle lines.

Trench life was not as tolerable as Lewis's letters home to his
father suggested, because by the end of January or beginning of
February, Lewis was hospitalized for three weeks at Le Tréport,
miles away from the front line, with trench fever or, more techni-
cally, PUO (pyrexia of unknown origin).

The Battle of Hazebrouck

It was not until the end of February that Lewis rejoined his battalion at Fampoux, a village to the west of Arras. He was now in the
direct line of the final German large-scale attack of the war on the
Western Front. Soon he had to spend a whole night digging, in
anticipation of the German advance southward. All hell broke loose
a little over two weeks later, on March 21, 1918. In the early hours
of that morning, German general Erich Ludendorff launched an

offensive designed to sweep the allied forces off the Western Front and to open the way for the capture of Paris. The initial softening-up bombardment lasted five hours.

A few days into the battle, elsewhere along the front, at Pargny, Paddy Moore was fighting with his 2nd Battalion of the Rifle Brigade, resisting the massive German offensive. He was last seen alive the morning of Sunday, March 24. His remains were taken up and buried in a field.[18] Mrs. Moore later was informed that he died from a bullet to the head as he was receiving emergency treatment for a wound. When this was happening, Lewis's battalion was being moved around the battlefront near Arras.

Between April 12 and 15, still in the area north of Arras, quite near the Belgian border, Lewis was caught up in the Battle of Hazebrouck. The action he saw took place around the village of Riez du Vinage. During the battle, much to his surprise, he took sixty retreating German prisoners who were eager to surrender. He was wounded on Monday April 15 by "friendly fire" at Mont-Bernenchon, a slightly elevated hamlet just southwest of Riez du Vinage. At least one British shell burst close by him, killing his friend Harry Ayres and fatally wounding Laurence Johnson, who were standing with him. Shards from the shell ripped into Lewis's body in three places, including his chest. Lewis then began to crawl back over the cold mud toward help and was picked up by a stretcher bearer. Within a couple of days Albert in Belfast received a telegram from the War Office: "2ND. LT. C. S. LEWIS SOMERSET LIGHT INFANTRY WOUNDED APRIL FIFTEENTH."[19] Pieces of shrapnel remained in his chest for much of his life.

Warren, stationed at Doullens, heard from Albert Lewis that his brother was wounded and hospitalized at Etaples (south of Boulogne, on the French coast). He borrowed a motorcycle and found his way the fifty miles west to the coastal hospital. Warnie was seized by anxiety as he drove. His fear turned to thankfulness and joy when he came across "Jacks" sitting up in bed. Though serious,

Warren found, the wounds were not life-threatening.

From the Liverpool Merchants Mobile Hospital at Etaples, a few days later, Lewis wrote to his father that he had been hit in the back of the left hand, on the left leg a little above the knee and in the left side under the armpit. Army medical records recorded, "Foreign body still present in chest, removal not contemplated—there is no danger to nerve or bone in other wounds."[20]

In the mobile hospital in Etaples, Lewis worked at understanding his hellish experience in the light of his atheistic beliefs. He sought to retain a place for beauty and the spirit in his materialist worldview (that is, the view that nature is the whole show—there is nothing outside it).[21] He thought about the "lusts of the flesh," which so often buffeted him. He had found himself to become almost monastic about them. This is because, he reasoned, fleshly desires increased the mastery of matter over the human spirit. On the battlefield, and in the hospital among the casualties of war, he saw spirit constantly evading matter—evading bullets, artillery shells, and driven by the sheer animal fears and pains that wrack human beings. He saw the equation starkly now as matter equals nature, equals Satan. The only nonnatural, nonmaterial thing that he discovered was beauty. Beauty was the only spiritual thing he could find. It was beauty versus nature, beauty versus Satan. Nature was a prison house from which only humans were capable of escape, through their spiritual side. There was however no God to aid them. It was a materialist's mysticism. It might seem odd to say this, but, in fact, in his mystical concerns as an avowed atheist, Lewis anticipated a feature of spirituality now commonplace in the West. With the increased influence, for instance, of Eastern thought, it has become clear that mysticisms have long existed outside of theistic beliefs—that is, beliefs in a God responsible for the existence of the universe, as found in Judaism, Christianity and Islam. The nontheistic mysticisms are found in Hinduism, Buddhism and many other beliefs.[22]

A poem called "Satan Speaks," from Lewis's volume of poetry composed in the war years, *Spirits in Bondage*, vividly portrays his atheist beliefs at this time:

I am the battle's filth and strain,

I am the widow's empty pain.

. . .

I am the fact and the crushing reason

To thwart your fantasy's new-born treason.[23]

Recovery and Convalescence

Lewis was transported in May 1918 to the Endsleigh Palace Hospital in central London. He was pleased to find this a comfortable place, where he even had a separate room. He was also happily aware of the fact that he could easily order from the many bookshops nearby.

Lewis arranged to continue his convalescence in Bristol, to be near Mrs. Moore and Maureen, being moved there near the end of June. His recovery was slower than anticipated—he remained in Bristol until mid-October. While in Bristol, Lewis was able to report some good news to his Ulster friend Arthur Greeves. After keeping his slim typescript of poetry for what seemed to him a considerable time, William Heinemann had accepted it for publication. Lewis told Arthur that it would be called *Spirits in Prison*, and that it was weaved around his belief that nature is a prison house and satanic. The spiritual—and God, should he exist—oppose "the cosmic arrangement." The book was eventually published under the revised title of *Spirits in Bondage* in March 1919, when Lewis was twenty.

Though war ended on November 11, 1918, Lewis was still on active service. Two days before Christmas, Warren arrived home in Belfast on leave. He believed that he would not see his brother, who was still at a military camp. But late on December 27 he recorded in his diary the unexpected arrival of Jack: "A red letter day. We were sitting in the study about eleven o'clock this morning when we saw a cab coming up the avenue." His brother had been demobilized.[24]

Another War, A Different C. S. Lewis

"My memories of the last war haunted my dreams for years." Lewis disclosed this in a letter over twenty years later, on May 8, 1939. War had become for him a deeply embedded image of a grimly persistent cosmic war between good and evil. In a sermon, "Learning in War-Time," written soon after the start of the new world war, he observed, "War creates no absolutely new situation; it simply aggravates the permanent human situation so that we can no longer ignore it."[25] During the years of the First World War and immediately after it, the struggle for him was conceived in terms of a battle between nature and spirit, with nature being evil unless touched by beauty and spirit. Bluntly, nature was Satan, the devil. After Lewis's conversion to theism around the end of the 1920s and to Christian belief in 1931, he accepted an orthodox (or, as he was fond of saying, a "mere") Christian view of the essential goodness of nature, in which evil is a despoiling and absence of good. Nature was spoiled, not evil in essence. Furthermore evil damaged both nature and spirit, with the origin of evil lying in our human freedom to rebel against God, rather than in nature itself. Lewis's war experience effectively became part of his inner life, first as a materialistic vision of the war of nature and spirit, and then as a cosmic battle between good and evil in Jewish-Christian terms. Lewis, even as an atheist, never indulged in the fashionable literary spirit of disillusionment after World War I. There was no fundamental mismatch between his beliefs and the horrors of his wartime experience.[26]

The start of the Second World War on Sunday, September 3, 1939, therefore found a C. S. Lewis who in many ways was different from the young man who tried to turn his experience of war into poetry. He had become a Christian just eight years before, after a long conversation with his friends J. R. R. Tolkien and "Hugo" Dyson and many conversations before that with Tolkien and also Barfield. His wide reading of Christian writers such as G. K. Chesterton, James Balfour and George MacDonald (not to mention seventeenth-century English poets) also played an important part. He increasingly valued his friends. Since becoming a Fellow and Tutor of Magdalen College, Oxford, in 1925, he had joined university clubs and surrounded himself with them. One group of friends who were inclined to write became around 1933 a literary club dubbed "the Inklings," of which Lewis was the life and soul and natural leader.[27] It took its name perhaps in the fall of that year, some months after Lewis published his first fiction, *The Pilgrim's Regress.* By then he and Tolkien had shared with each other manuscripts they were writing, and this habit carried over into the Inklings' meetings. Before the Inklings took shape Lewis already had been among the first to read an emerging draft of what became *The Hobbit* (not published until 1937). Tolkien subsequently read at least some of the book to the Inklings. In that book, evil is portrayed by a traditional dragon straight out of Old Norse mythology—its darker representation as a crafted ring is only in seed form. There is, however, in the background, the shadowy figure of the Necromancer, who is revealed in the later sequel *The Lord of the Rings* to be Sauron, the Dark Lord.

For all the differences between the young schoolboy and then subaltern in World War I and the Oxford Don just in his forties in World War II, the younger and older Lewis were united in perceiving war as a symbol of the permanent human condition. But whereas Satan as a symbol equaled nature, equaled the enemy of the spirit in the First War, in the Second, Lewis saw him as the real implacable foe of the embodied human being—a human being who is both physical and mental-spiritual. The devil was still a key to understanding how evil worked, but now it was evil as a parasite on and perversion of spiritual and natural good, rather than one side of a dualism, where the material world pitted itself against human spiritual longings. Evil is always a pressing question, Lewis was convinced, but world war made it inescapable. In fact, modern, total war was a creative matrix of not only Lewis's work but also books and other writings by fellow Inklings that explored devilry and its effects on human beings. Most famously the output of the group included *The Screwtape Letters* and *The Lord of the Rings*, but also the less known novel of Charles Williams, *All Hallows Eve*, admired by T. S. Eliot (who knew Williams of old, but more recently had become acquainted with Lewis). Eliot remarked of Williams, "He could have joked with the devil and turned the joke against him."[28] The war was also reflected in the conversations of the Inklings as many of these works in progress were read to the circle.

The war made many demands and required sacrifices. Warren Lewis was recalled at the beginning of war in 1939 to military service on account of his previous professional career in the British Army, but Lewis and most of his Inklings friends were deemed too old or physically unfit to serve. Many of them were, like Lewis, scarred by war and felt obliged to make their own war effort. Lewis expressed this in a number of ways, including the subject of much of his writing during that golden period of the Inklings. But the opening of the war gave him an immediate opportunity to do something. Like Professor Kirke in *The Lion, the Witch and the Wardrobe*, he took in evacuees from London in danger of bombing by enemy action.

The Evacuees, and Patrolling Oxford

Since the beginning of the 1930s Lewis had lived with Mrs. Janie Moore (the mother of Paddy Moore) and her daughter Maureen in The Kilns, a red brick bungalow-style house on the edge of Oxford.

The children in the first batch to come to The Kilns, all girls, brought little with them—a gas mask, in a large box attached to a shoulder strap, spare clothing, a toothbrush, comb, handkerchief and a bag of food for the day they traveled. Lewis, whose experience of children up to this time was quite limited, instantly warmed to the young lodgers.

The evacuees, coming from cities, had little or no experience of the countryside. The Kilns, on the rural fringe of Oxford and in its ample grounds, soon came to resemble to some extent a small-holding, and this resemblance deepened as the war progressed. The low, rambling brick house was set in eight acres of land, which in-cluded a tennis court, an apple orchard, a pond in the nearby woodland and many hens. Eggs were on the menu everyday. There were hen coops and rabbit cages to be cleaned.

The impact of the evacuees on Lewis carried over into his writing, which was to touch the lives of readers and film audiences around the globe in later years. Soon after the first children arrived, he started to write a story, soon abandoned, which had at its center four evacuee children. Lewis would pick up the story again in 1949, and it became the first story of Narnia, *The Lion, the Witch and the Wardrobe*, in which children enter another, magical world through an old wardrobe.

The story connected the events of wartime England with a battle against an ancient evil in Narnia, as those evacuee children help loyal Narnian talking beasts to overcome the power of the White Witch, who has placed their lush wooded country under a curse of perpetual winter. Though the story was written after the Second World War, its setting is firmly within it, the threat of Nazi bombing causing the Pevensie children to be evacuated to Professor Kirke's country house. Curiously, the story also linked one wartime with another in Lewis's mind. In mid-November 1914, not long after Lewis had started to be tutored by W. T. Kirkpatrick in Surrey (who partly inspired Professor Kirke), and soon after going to see the evacuated Belgian family, he had visited a snowy wood.

Bookham had been coated with a deep fall of snow. The transformed landscape awakened the boy's imagination. The nearby pine wood, particularly, wowed him. It had white snow masses on trees and ground, forming what he described in a letter to Arthur Greeves as a "beautiful sight." He almost expected, he said, a hasty "march of dwarfs" to pass, breaking the stillness. Many years later, Lewis remembered about the origin of Narnia: "The Lion [the Witch and the Wardrobe] all began with a picture of a Faun carrying an umbrella and parcels in a snowy wood. This picture had been in my mind since I was about sixteen. Then one day, when I was about forty, I said to myself: 'Let's try to make a story about it.'"[29] It is quite possible that the snowy wood near Bookham stimulated the mental picture, given that it was natural for him to imagine dwarfs passing through the trees. The experience in the woodland occurred around the time of his sixteenth birthday, which correlates with Lewis's memory.

C. S. Lewis, like many of his age, served during the Second World War in the Local Defence Volunteers, later renamed the Home Guard, or "Dad's Army," as it was nicknamed, fulfilling a variety of duties. The Volunteers were formed when the threat of invasion, including paratroopers from the skies, was acute. Tolkien served in a different role, on fire-watch duties. One clear night in 1940, Tolkien noticed a strong and strange light growing and spreading over the northern horizon. Next day he learned it was the burning of Coventry forty or so miles to the north—Oxford escaped the blitz. When Lewis's brother, Warren, eventually was discharged from military service, he also served with the Home Guard, utilizing his boat on Oxford's waterways.

The Impact of War on C. S. Lewis's Writings

Leading up to the war, during and immediately after it, C. S. Lewis explored themes of heaven and hell, modern and ancient evil, devilry and a form of purgatory in a variety of books, both fiction and non-fiction. These are best understood against the context of the time and at least in part the influence of Charles Williams as well as his other friends such as Tolkien. These years of war saw his increasing popularly as a speaker and writer on Christianity, as in his enormously popular broadcast talks for BBC Radio, and, of course, can be seen in the origins of the rather academic devil, Screwtape, who was born in the context of Lewis's wartime concerns.[30]

Noticeable is Tolkien and Lewis's perception of a devilish plot against humanity with the machine and applied science as the modern form of magic. Though Lewis makes passing references to technological devilry and explores it in his third science-fiction story, *That Hideous Strength*, he made his concerns very explicit in his inaugural lecture as Professor of Medieval and Renaissance Literature in Cambridge, which was not until 1954. The intellectual climate that gives rise to and allows a technology cast off from the values of humanity as it has been understood for a vast period of time, however, was the subject of Lewis's wartime philosophical essay *The Abolition of Man*. Some of Tolkien's rather similar reflections on the subject are to be found scattered in his correspondence, often expounding *The Lord of the Rings* to interested readers. For instance, he revealed his understanding that Sauron's Ring was essentially a machine made to objectify his power. He described the current war in one letter to his son, Christopher Tolkien, as "the first War of the Machines."[31] He also said of the war in another letter, "we are attempting to conquer Sauron with the Ring. And we shall (it seems) succeed. But the penalty is, you will know, to breed new Saurons, and slowly turn Men and Elves into Orcs."[32]

Lewis's books on devilry had behind them, or focused on, damnation or salvation in the moral choices of human being. Through a carefully presented argument *The Problem of Pain* brought in issues of animal suffering, the terrors of hell and the joy of heaven. Lewis started writing the book just before the outbreak of war, and it was no mere abstract treatise. More scholarly books were not exempted from a theme of devilry. Lewis's study of and introduction to Milton's *Paradise Lost* appeared two years later, in 1942—a Christian epic that has influenced contemporary writers as diverse as Lewis himself and the atheist Philip Pullman. As well as a brilliant defense of the poem, building on insights of Charles Williams on Milton, Lewis expounds on ascending levels or hierarchy in the created world, including the realm of the devil and angelic beings. Lewis's imaginative counterpart to this study of Milton, appearing a year later, was his second science-fiction story, *Perelandra* (also called *Voyage to Venus*), which we shall look at in chapter six. Here the story of Adam and Eve is enacted on another planet, in which a surprising hero, the linguist Dr. Elwin ("Elf-Friend") Ransom, is carried to Venus from Earth to intervene in helping to thwart devilry there.

His most famous treatment of the conflict between good and evil was also written amid the uncertainties of a world at war. This is the story, mentioned earlier, that had come to Lewis in the quiet of his local church on a Sunday morning as the aerial Battle of Britain raged in summer 1940. It would give one side of the correspondence between the retired senior devil, Screwtape, and his inexperienced nephew, Wormwood. This was *The Screwtape Letters*.

2

Devilry and the Problem of Hell

The Screwtape Letters

There is a young man—we do not know his name—who lives in a large town or city in England. He is someone that you wouldn't look at twice if you passed him in the street. He lives with his increasingly garrulous mother. As the Second World War approaches he becomes a Christian, and then agonizes over whether to fight or to become a pacifist. He struggles with his newfound faith, not least in the tensions that exist between himself and his mother. He falls in with a smart set of worldly-wise friends with whom his Christian faith jars (so much so that he keeps quiet about it, simply showing that a Christian can be a fine fellow). Partly as a result, the initial ardor of his faith begins to cool. When he falls in love with a devout young Christian woman, this marks a new step in his devotion to God, even though he continues to experience the common trials and tests of faith. With the onset of enemy bombing he becomes an air raid warden and soon witnesses firsthand the horror and terror of modern warfare as he comes across death and shattered human remains. Before long he himself dies on duty as a result of a bomb blast.

On the face of it, this is what C. S. Lewis's *The Screwtape Letters* is about—an ordinary, unheroic life of someone who, nevertheless, courageously faces the horror of war, in which civilians are in the front line. What Lewis does, however, is to tell a wider story of what lies behind, above and below the apparently simple events from the brief life. Lewis chronicles the salvation and attempted damnation of that young man and much else from the point of view of hell. It's simple in the story—bad equals good; the perspective is inverted, gaining plausibility from the urbane voice of the academically inclined Screwtape. As Lewis explained, "Screwtape's outlook is like a photographic negative; his whites are all blacks and whatever he welcomes we ought to dread."[1] The slanted story unfolds in the one side of a correspondence we read between a senior and a junior devil, whose relationship approximates to that of uncle and nephew. Attestations of affection by the uncle for his nephew turn out in the end to be a hunger to devour him, and the bonds between demons are not of love but of fear and a ravenous mutual hunger on which their existence depends. Lewis's purpose is not to exaggerate the role of the devil and devilry in human affairs, but to highlight the eternal seriousness of our moral dilemmas as humans from a startling perspective. Concerning overinterest in demons he points out, "Our attitude should be that of the sensible citizen in wartime who believes that there are enemy spies in our midst but disbelieves nearly every particular spy story."[2]

The fairly nondescript life of the young man (bureaucratically called "the Patient" by the senior devil, Screwtape) actually turns out to be full of drama, gripped by the cosmic conflict of good and evil, as well as by the seeming idiocy of death and destruction handed out by earthly war.

Screwtape's weekly epistles to his nephew, Wormwood, present a picture of the powerful reach of hell and its diabolical ways that turns out to be much more than the traditional iconography of Milton's *Paradise Lost*, the mystery plays, Dante and medieval poetry, even though that is very much present. What Lewis does not do is to speculate about what actually goes on in hell (which he believed to be real)—he has no desire to feed or inflame any curiosity in that regard the reader may have. Rather he employs what he liked to call a "supposal," a kind of "what if" that is at the heart of imaginative storytelling. "What if" hell resembled a cross between a ruthless modern company and a police state? Suppose hell echoes the bureaucracy and efficiency of Hitler's fascist Reich and that incipient tendency, Lewis believed, in all modern states—states that belong to the current "Age of the Machine." Interestingly, a similar idea about hell was in Owen Barfield's mind around this time. Barfield, friend and fellow Inkling, wrote a poetic play, *Orpheus*, in 1937 at Lewis's suggestion, which was not performed until many years later in 1949. In his *The Magical World of the Inklings*, Gareth Knight comments on a scene in hell, "Hades, which we enter with Orpheus in Act III, is rather like an efficient corporation or corporate state in the world we know. All the denizens are persuaded into thinking that they live in the best of all possible worlds and that they should be grateful for their hellish lot."[3]

The Screwtape Letters is the most obvious of books about devilry that C. S. Lewis wrote, and it was the book he found most unpleasant to write. The book is a comical and satirical look at that most serious of subjects, damnation. The letters first appeared in a weekly religious journal called *The Guardian* between May 2 and November 28, 1941. Screwtape is a senior presence in the Lowerarchy of hell, and his letters of advice and warning are directed to a trainee tempter. Wormwood, fresh from the Tempter's Training College, has been assigned a "Patient," and his task is to secure his damnation. It was unfortunate for Wormwood that his client soon becomes a Christian. Uncle Screwtape passes on a number of useful suggestions for reclaiming the young man. These come both from his centuries of experience and from information from hell's Intelligence Department, with its vast databank of files on every human.

Screwtape is also in touch with other tempters assigned to the patient's friends, acquaintances and relations. Wormwood particularly sees great possibilities in the person of the young man's very trying mother. The "Patient" successfully avoids the pull of those worldly friends whom the junior tempter employs in his cause.

Wormwood faces hell and his uncle's ravenous hunger when, first, his Patient falls in love with the devout Christian and, second, when he fails to keep the young man out of the danger of death, is killed in an air raid and is forever put out of the reach of hell's clutches. The idea had been to restore the Patient to a damned state in the more conducive context of a comfortable life and cushioned decline in old age. Screwtape's consolation lies in devouring at least a morsel of his bungling nephew.

One reviewer at the time the book came out remarked that he hoped the tempter assigned to him was as incompetent as Wormwood rather than as capable and successful as Screwtape. *The Screwtape Letters* turned out to be one of C. S. Lewis's most popular books, earning him the accolade of eventually being featured on the cover of *Time* magazine during September 1947.

Lewis deliberately gives Screwtape a certain twisted eminence in his belief that greater beings are capable of greater evil. Indeed, as an academic of sorts, Screwtape at times sounds rather like Lewis himself when you read the prose of, say, *Mere Christianity* or *The Problem of Pain*, which was a deliberate choice of voice by the author. Interestingly, Screwtape admits hell's lack of power against its ultimate "Enemy," but continues to trust optimistically in its bureaucracy and utter "realism" about the Enemy's true motives, even though some motives Screwtape admits have not yet been understood. He relishes any opportunity to deconstruct seemingly selfless claims such as those of love. Any gain by one being is strictly numerical—it is at the expense of another. Self-sacrifice is a sham, in Screwtape's view.

One of the most important devices of hell in the present age, as we learn through Screwtape, is its concealment and subterfuge. The temptations and prodding of humans—indeed all truly successful devilry—is best when it is no more noticeable than settled weather. Diabolical tactics as presented by Screwtape are actually rather similar to those of spies, as expressed by an author Lewis enjoyed, John Buchan, in the famous Richard Hannay story *The Thirty-Nine Steps*. Hannay recalls something he once heard in Africa from his old Boer friend Peter Pienaar about the successful spy.

> He laughed at things like dyed hair and false beards and such childish follies. The only thing that mattered was what Peter called "atmosphere."
>
> If a man could get into perfectly different surroundings from those in which he had been first observed, and—this is the important part—really play up to these surroundings and behave as if he had never been out of them, he would puzzle the cleverest detectives on earth. And he used to tell a story of how he once borrowed a black coat and went to church and shared the same hymn-book with the man that was looking for him. If that man had seen him in decent company before he would have recognized him; but he had only seen him snuffing the lights in a public-house with a revolver.
>
> The recollection of Peter's talk gave me the first real comfort that I had had that day. Peter had been a wise old bird, and these fellows I was after were about the pick of the aviary. What if they were playing Peter's game? A fool tries to look different: a clever man looks the same and is different.[4]

The unsuccessful "spy" in *The Screwtape Letters* is the young tempter, Wormwood, whom his uncle fruitlessly encourages not to alert his Patient to his malevolent presence.

Another (but related) way of expressing this tactic of concealment is in terms of plausibility—referring to that which fits the ambience of a period. Screwtape's argument for effective devilry is that of avoiding matters of truth and reason. The aim, rather, is a comfortable (and comforting) plausibility. His key strategy is in effect to foster a reliance on subjective thoughts and feelings, those we feel comfortable with and that do not disturb our inner equilibrium—those that are not exposed to the gaze of others or tested or allowed to be judged by conscience or objective knowledge, or unfamiliar or unwelcome ideas. An extreme example is the idea that we are never going to die.

The contrast between this comfortable kind of plausibility and truth itself, as set out by Lewis, may be illustrated, I think, in current views of the origin of the universe. In many parts of the world in the twenty-first century it is plausible to believe in a divine Creator of the universe. In other parts, where it is often a mark of secularism, it is plausible to see the universe as having a purely material origin, in being self-created.[5] It begins with nothing and ends in nothing. Unfortunately it is often the case that both the secular and the supernatural views of origin rest on what is felt to be plausible rather than what is rigorously thought to be truth. Screwtape was worried that if the focus shifted away from the comfortably plausible to the question of what is true, then those they were intent on trapping would be on "Enemy" ground and therefore in grave danger of being lost to them. The harvest of souls would be diminished, and it may be that a particularly choice meal may be lost. The philosopher Nietzsche prophetically commented, "What is now decisive against Christianity is our taste, no longer our reasons."[6]

Screwtape's ravenous hunger has already been mentioned. Hunger and food in fact dominate the Lowerarchy of hell, witnessed by constant references in *The Screwtape Letters* (and also the later "Screwtape Proposes a Toast"). In fact, food and hunger provide a master image holding together the symbolism of devilry in the book.

Lewis calls it "spiritual cannibalism," and says he may have obtained the idea from disturbing sequences of absorption in a science-fiction story that was a major influence on his own fiction—David Lindsay's *Voyage to Arcturus.*[7] Whereas the "Enemy" desires the "human vermin" (as Screwtape calls us) to love him and each other, the "austerity" and "dignity" of hell require absolute self-interest, with none of the self-surrender and humility of love for another.

The passion that motivated hell is, and can only be, hunger and its satisfaction at the expense of others. Not only does Screwtape hunger to devour humans captured by devilry, but, like all his diabolical kin, also desires to gorge himself on his fellow demons, where this is permitted. He signs himself throughout "Your affectionate uncle, Screwtape." The reader gradually realizes that *affection* is one of numerous words skewed by hell into a very different meaning; in the regions below it means acute hunger to devour another. When Wormwood finally loses his charge to heaven, he is fair game for consumption as an incompetent tempter. Screwtape accordingly signs his final letter, "Your increasingly and ravenously affectionate uncle Screwtape."

Lewis picks up this theme of insatiable hunger bonding those on devilish intent in his final science-fiction story, *That Hideous Strength*, which we shall look at in chapter six. In the abandonment of their humanity, Lewis is implying, there is no other bond. Two members of the sinister N.I.C.E. (National Institute of Co-ordinated Experiments), Professor Frost—apparently a psychologist—and Deputy Director Wither are pictured at one point drawing close like lovers in their unspoken hunger to assimilate each other, just as Screwtape desires his bungling nephew. One of them gradually draws his chair closer to the other as they discuss the fate of Jane Studdock, gifted with second sight, whom they seek to capture via her husband, Mark.

They were now sitting so close together that their faces almost touched, as if they had been lovers about to kiss. Frost's *pince-nez* caught the light so that they made his eyes invisible: only his mouth, smiling but not relaxed in the smile, revealed his expression. Wither's mouth was open, the lower lip hanging down, his eyes wet, his whole body hunched and collapsed in his chair as if the strength had gone out of it. A stranger would have thought he had been drinking. Then his shoulders twitched and gradually he began to laugh. . . . With sudden swift convulsive movement, the two old men lurched forward towards each other and sat swaying to and fro, locked in an embrace from which each seemed to be struggling to escape. And as they swayed and scrabbled with hand and nail, there arose, shrill and faint at first, but then louder and louder, a cackling noise that seemed in the end rather an animal than a senile parody of laughter.[8]

The banality and dehumanizing effect of entrenched devilry is beautifully captured in this incident.

In the later "Screwtape Proposes a Toast," where Screwtape is guest of honor at the Tempters' Training College annual dinner, he in his banquet speech refers to the poor quality of that year's damned: "Oh, to get one's teeth again into a Farinata, a Henry VIII or even a Hitler! There was real crackling there; something to crunch; a rage, an egotism, a cruelty only just less robust than our own. It put up a delicious resistance to being devoured. It warmed your inwards when you'd got it down." Though the reader laughs and enjoys the satire and irony here, the moral seriousness of what Lewis is writing is not weakened. It is, rather, strengthened. As the eminent philosopher and broadcaster C. E. M. Joad observed in his review of *The Screwtape Letters*, "Mr Lewis possesses the rare gift of being able to make righteousness readable."[9]

C. S. Lewis had been glad to cast aside *The Screwtape Letters*, now free of putting himself within the reverse perspective of hell's agents upon ordinary human life. The letters had been very firmly focused on someone who appeared rather nondescript, as we saw—the young man who gets caught up in war. An invitation for a story a number of years later from America's *Saturday Evening Post* gave him an opportunity to return briefly to Screwtape's view of the world. In "Screwtape Proposes a Toast," Screwtape gives the speech at the Tempters' Training College. The focus of the distinguished demon's banquet speech is on society, and in particular education, but pointing out dangers of complacency over ensuring human damnation.

The College is where junior devils learn their skills in damning human beings, or in attempting to reclaim those who have gone over to "the Enemy." After graduation, novices apparently have practical experience under the guidance of an experienced devil. In *The Screwtape Letters*, Wormwood is a recent graduate mentored by Screwtape.

The fundamental tactic that Screwtape is urging on the newly graduated devils in "Screwtape Proposes a Toast" is to muddy the concept of democracy in education. (This is part of a wider diabolical strategy to destroy the humanity of people—the subject of Lewis's philosophical essay on education, *The Abolition of Man* [see appendix 2], published just a year after *The Screwtape Letters*, on January 6, 1943.)[10] In his preface to the new edition of *The Screwtape Letters*, which includes Screwtape's banquet speech, Lewis outlines the main point that Screwtape insists demons must obscure and muddle in human minds:

> There is a sense in which education ought to be democratic and another sense in which it ought not. It ought to be democratic in the sense of being available, without distinction of sex, colour, class, race or religion, to all who can—and will—

diligently accept it. But once the young people are inside the school there must be no attempt to establish a factitious egalitarianism between the idlers and dunces on the one hand and the clever and industrious on the other. A modern nation needs a very large class of genuinely educated people and it is the primary function of schools to supply them. To lower standards or disguise inequalities is fatal.[11]

The diabolical sense of "democracy" in fact becomes, in Screwtape's words, "*I'm as good as you*, Being like Folks, Togetherness."[12] Hell, says the banquet speaker, "would welcome the disappearance of democracy in the strict sense of that word, the political arrangement so called."[13] "*I'm as good as you*" has a greater value even than the destruction of democratic societies, argues Screwtape, "as a state of mind which, necessarily excluding humility, charity, contentment, and all the pleasures of gratitude or admiration, turns a human being away from almost every road which might finally lead him to Heaven."[14]

In writing for *The Saturday Evening Post*, Lewis displays a remarkable knowledge of the American public school system, and peppers his prose with Americanisms such as "all-right Joes," "bums," "Graft sauce" and "crooner." It seems possible that Lewis's American wife, Joy Davidman, collaborated in creating "Screwtape Proposes a Toast," just as, in earlier years, Lewis had asked her novelist opinion on his initial drafts of his story *Till We Have Faces*.[15] Tactfully, Lewis writes about education as if Screwtape were alluding to England, leaving it to smart readers to make the connection with US public education.

Lewis's Approach to the Devil

C. S. Lewis's view of a personal devil in *The Screwtape Letters* comes over clearly, not lost in the satirical genre that he employs. His belief is based on the ground that supernatural beings exist, a view that is rationally defensible and does not conflict philosophically with endorsing the enterprise of science. Though considered by Lewis not to be among the best of his books, it stands in a long line of books concerned with angels, demons and spiritual powers, such as Dante's *Divine Comedy* (fourteenth century), Milton's *Paradise Lost* (1667, 1674) and John Macgowan's satirical *Infernal Conference; or Dialogues of Devils* (1772).[16] This genre is still very much alive in the twenty-first century. Lewis famously remarks in his original preface: "There are two equal and opposite errors into which our race can fall about the devils. One is to disbelieve in their existence. The other is to believe, and to feel an excessive and unhealthy interest in them. They themselves are equally pleased with both errors, and hail a materialist or a magician with the same delight."

Though Lewis may never have read it (though he appears to have heard of it), Reverend John Macgowan's *Dialogues of Devils* expands on his point.[17] (Interestingly that book has a demon, Fastosus, who is uncle of another devil, Avaro, and represents the inverse perspective of hell by reporting the overheard conversations of demons.) Macgowan writes like Lewis in his introduction of the two extremes of opinion about devils:

> Nothing can be more various and opposite than the opinions of mankind respecting the influence and agency of infernal spirits. Some continually throw the blame of their vices on the poor devil;—take their word for it, and they are upon all occasions the innocent dupes to his subtlety and malice; they represent him as the prime agent in all their complicated schemes of wickedness; and would fain persuade us, that so far from being the objects of our just aversion, they deserve all our commiseration and pity. From such representations one would be tempted to think, that if malicious and busy devils did but stay in their own country, mankind would be as

harmless as lambs and every species of wickedness be soon
banished from our then agreeable world.

Others there be who fall into the opposite extreme, and
with all their power endeavor to clear the Devil of the slanders
thrown upon him; whether he hath retained them as his ad-
vocates, I pretend not to say: but they tell you that he has no
hand in all the wickedness committed under the sun; that it
is impossible he should have any influence on the minds and
manners of men. Nay, some go farther still, even doubt of his
very existence, and are confident that all their wickedness
ariseth from another quarter.[18]

Like Macgowan, C. S. Lewis was determined to avoid either error.
Yet as he thought and wrote much about the issue of evil in the dark
years of World War II, and as he tried out thoughts and writings
with his group of Inklings friends, the part of the devil, and devilry,
had to be considered. The devil, he saw, was neither the eternal opposite of God, matching his power in constant conflict, nor to be
removed from a proper narrative of human history (at least in respect of there being fallen angels—devils—active in events on Earth).
Fantasy proved to be a fitting mode to capture Satan's elusive person
(it has been remarked that Satan lacks a face in his fictional appearances), as it was to explore the enigmas of evil. Images of evil teemed
in his imagination, as they did in Tolkien's and Charles Williams's.

But Lewis did not think of devilry only in philosophical terms or
in connection with great evils like the deliberate destruction of
large swaths of innocent civilians. *The Screwtape Letters* is firmly
focused on the details of ordinary life and the fate of a seemingly
insignificant young man. Screwtape himself regards the World War
raging in the 1940s almost as a distraction from the serious business
of damnation, even though it was a great source of pleasure to him
and his colleagues in hell. In his biography of C. S. Lewis, A. N.

Wilson brilliantly describes Lewis's ability to capture the comic dramas of ordinary life, which are so evident in *The Screwtape Letters*. Wilson points out that Lewis was schooled in such observations by his father, Albert, who was full of what Lewis and his brother called "wheezes," humorous stories from events he had witnessed, and by Mrs. Janie Moore, the single parent Lewis effectively adopted as his mother. Wilson argues that Lewis's years with Mrs. Moore had a dramatic influence on his writing—it may be his writings without her might have been more prolific and scholarly in character, but lacking the kind of books that made him popular, such as *The Screwtape Letters* and *Mere Christianity*:

> He is the great chronicler of the minor domestic irritation, of the annoying little trait bulking to (literally) hellish proportions. Domestic life with his father had been the training-school for this distinctly Lewisian vision. Minto [Mrs. Moore] not only provided him with plenty of *Screwtape*-style domestic situations. She also had a rich enjoyment of the comedy of human character, which was one of the things she shared with Lewis.[19]

Wilson characterizes Lewis's perception of domestic life as misanthropic in tendency, perhaps fueled by Mrs. Moore's way of seeing things. However, this is speculation that does not illuminate *The Screwtape Letters.* There Lewis's portrayals of tiny aspects of domestic situations are in fact realistic about the processes of sin and damnation, striking a chord with his many readers.[20] In Lewis, indeed, the devil is in the details. The domestic vignettes are in the firm context of the skewed perspective of hell, providing an artistic distance that allows recognition and what Lewis called "undeception" in his reader (see chap. 10). Here is just one brief example from Letter III, where uncle Screwtape, who certainly is misanthropic, writes,

Since his ideas about [his mother's] soul will be very crude and often erroneous, he will, in some degree, be praying for an imaginary person, and it will be your task to make that imaginary person daily less and less like the real mother—the sharp-tongued old lady at the breakfast table.

Lewis's guiding insight that the road to hell is paved with small, seemingly insignificant decisions is one he shared with Charles Williams. In the latter's novel *Descent into Hell* (1937), Lawrence Wentworth, a historian, slowly "descends into hell" as a result of forcing historical facts to fit his opinions. Small lies and minor choices that seem inevitable seamlessly lead him to damnation. On one occasion he is consulted over historical costumes to be used in a masque, and cheats by saying that they are correct although he knows they are not, in fact, in a detail. Like voices in a megaphone, selfish and manipulative choices are grossly magnified in events Wentworth becomes caught up in. Both Lewis and Williams believed that the same principle applied in the journey to heaven rather than hell. In Williams's last novel, *All Hallows Eve* (1945), which was read in installments to the Inklings, the simplest human acts of kindness and love become powerful images of salvation in the struggle against the perverted spiritual power of Simon the Clerk.

Telling a Story Through Letters

The determined, sharp focus of the narrator, Screwtape, on ordinary life at a definite time (the war years) is in keeping with the genre that Lewis chose for *The Screwtape Letters*. The epistolary story goes back to the early novels of the eighteenth century, with Samuel Richardson's *Pamela* and Henry Fielding's parody on it, *Shamela*, or Johann Wolfgang von Goethe's *Die Leiden des jungen Werthers* (*The Sorrows of Young Werther*). It was a versatile form of narrative, with a first-person point of view, but relating to the recipient of the letters, and sometimes including letters from others. Late in life Lewis composed another book made up of one side of a correspondence (*Letters to Malcolm: Chiefly on Prayer*), but there is less of an overarching story line than in *The Screwtape Letters*.

In choosing this genre Lewis cleverly allows the reader to step into the reverse perspective of hell, which is central to the effectiveness of the book. The wittiness of this device is sustained by the cleverness of the narrator, Screwtape, who is something of an academic as we saw, a little like Lewis himself. Lewis was well aware of the importance of writing from a world familiar to an author! When it came to a familiarity with the processes of temptation, Lewis confessed that he had only to examine his own heart to discover these. As the process gave him a kind of spiritual "cramp," as he put it, he was glad to leave the writing.

The resolution of the story with the death of the young man in the air raid, and the failure of hell's powers to snatch him back into the clutches of hell, vividly evokes the wartime setting. It is a dual setting, for there is both the earthly war between 1939 and 1945, and the spiritual conflict between good and evil powers. This double setting also marks the real lives of the Inklings during this period.

3

Inklings in Wartime

Themes of Spiritual Conflict

During World War II, perhaps not surprisingly, C. S. Lewis and his friends were particularly preoccupied with devilry and related issues like the lure of the dark side. This is apparent in many of their writings, where they picture human life finding its fulfillment through images of seeking heaven and shunning hell. The context of course is the battles and devastations of a global war. We shall look at a few of these writings in this chapter, and another of them, *The Great Divorce,* in chapter eight.

Only some of those who met in the more reading-based Inklings on Thursday evenings (or sometimes Fridays) actually wrote very much. Nevertheless, there were a good number of books published by Inklings members between 1939 and 1945, the war years (see the following list). Even then, before the war started, its imminence affected the mood of their country, and for several years afterwards there was painful adjustment and reconstruction. On a basic level, some rationing continued in Britain until 1954. Books published from 1939 to 1945 (in two cases drafted only at that time) are included. Here are some of their publications or broadcasts, most obviously relevant to the theme of goodness and evil, and are limited to those Inklings who attended meetings during the war years, so far as we know.[1]

The House by the Stable, Charles Williams (written 1939; published 1948 in *Seed of Adam and Other Plays*)
The Problem of Pain, C. S. Lewis, 1940
Witchcraft, Charles Williams, 1941
Grab and Grace, Charles Williams, 1941
The Screwtape Letters, C. S. Lewis, 1942
A Preface to Paradise Lost, C. S. Lewis, 1942
The Forgiveness of Sins, Charles Williams, 1942
Broadcast Talks, C. S. Lewis, 1942
The Three Temptations (BBC Radio Play), Charles Williams, 1942
Christian Behaviour, C. S. Lewis, 1943
Perelandra, C. S. Lewis, 1943
The Abolition of Man, C. S. Lewis, 1943
Beyond Personality, C. S. Lewis, 1944
That Hideous Strength, C. S. Lewis, 1945
The Great Divorce, C. S. Lewis, 1945
The House of the Octopus, Charles Williams, 1945
All Hallows Eve, Charles Williams, 1945

These actual publications only give part of a picture of their writings at this time. Lewis very briefly started out composing and then abandoned what would later become *The Lion, the Witch and the Wardrobe*, with its wartime setting of evacuees and its own enemy occupation in Narnia. During this period, J. R. R. Tolkien wrote much of *The Lord of the Rings* (not published until 1954–1955, and dedicated, in the first volume, to the Inklings). In the early 1940s, Owen Barfield was working on a dramatic trilogy titled "Angels at Bay," which was never published. This featured human characters on both sides of the threshold between this life and after death, and included angelic beings.[2]

Tolkien's preoccupation with events taking place around a world at war is sharply highlighted in a letter written to his son, Christopher, serving with the RAF. He wrote after the Nazi surrender "the War is not over (and the one that is, or the part of it, has largely been lost). But it is of course wrong to fall into such a mood, for Wars are always lost, and The War always goes on; and it is no good growing faint!"[3] By "The War" that "always goes on" he was referring to the spiritual battle against the powers of darkness.

World War II, of course, was a crisis for Western civilization. As Britain faced invasion by the Nazis, Churchill rallied the country to resist in robust terms, capturing and articulating its mood: "If we can stand up to [Hitler], all Europe may be freed and the life of the world may move forward into broad, sunlit uplands. But if we fail, then the whole world, . . . including all we have known and cared for, will sink into the abyss of a new Dark Age made more sinister, and perhaps more protracted, by the lights of perverted science."[4] An Oxford philosophy don, John D. Mabbott, later looked back to the earlier world war and contrasted it with the new one:

> In 1914 all the undergraduates, except a few invalids and foreigners, rushed to enlist, and by October Oxford was empty. The younger dons all joined up too. . . . In 1939 everything was completely different. The scientists were directed to complete their courses. For the Arts men, some academic work could be combined with military training for a year or so. It was not expected that a vast civilian army would be needed. Nor did it seem likely that the 300,000 casualties of Passchendaele would be repeated and a whole generation practically wiped out. So the Colleges went on at half strength in tutors and pupils.[5]

The wartime period was something of a golden age for the Inklings of Oxford. There were two important magical ingredients in the mix that created this uplift. One was the arrival of Charles Williams in Oxford on the heels of the outbreak of war in September 1939. He, together with other members of the London branch of the Oxford University Press, was evacuated to the mother city. The other ingredient was magic in its darkest form—the global war itself, fought with the most terrifying weapons modern technology could devise, devouring entire cities. The vitality of this period did not at first die with Charles Williams's sudden, unexpected death just after V-E Day in May 1945, but continued for several years more, until the demise, probably in autumn 1949, of the Inklings as a reading group made up of at least a core of writers. The group, however, still continued as a lively conversation group, and there were possibly readings on odd occasions after 1949.

"A Roaring Cataract of Nonsense"

A partly recorded meeting of the Inklings happened on November 9, 1939, less than two months after Charles Williams arrived on the scene. It illustrates the atmosphere of wartime Inklings sessions, at least the overtly literary ones.

Lewis's brother and fellow Inkling, Major W. H. "Warnie" Lewis, was, at that stage of the war, away from Oxford in France, having been recalled to military service despite his age. Like most members of the Inklings at that time he had served in the First World War, which ended just over twenty years before. Tolkien and Lewis, centerpieces of the group, and Charles Williams, who was soon to be valued as a central member, were not required to serve. Tolkien had even been told that he was not needed at that time for cryptography work. Warnie's absence did mean that his brother corresponded with him, which resulted in references to meetings of the Inklings in the letters. The gatherings themselves were not of course minuted.

In a lengthy letter to Warnie dated November 11, 1939, C. S. Lewis recorded his week and included a scene in his college rooms:

On Thursday we had a meeting of the Inklings—you and Coghill both absented unfortunately. I have never in my life seen Dyson so exuberant—"a roaring cataract of nonsense." The bill of fare afterwards [in Lewis's College rooms] consisted of a section of the new Hobbit book from Tolkien, a nativity play from Williams (unusually intelligible for him, and approved by all) and a chapter out of the book on the Problem of Pain from me. It so happened—it would take too long to explain why—that the subject matter of the three readings formed almost a logical sequence, and produced a really first rate evening's talk of the usual wide-ranging kind—"from grave to gay, from lively to severe." I wished very much we could have had you with us.[6]

The sequence of readings almost certainly all related to the nature of good and evil. We pretty much know the stage that Tolkien had reached at this time in writing *The Lord of the Rings*. We also know which play Williams had just written, and, of course, Lewis's *The Problem of Pain* is devoted to this issue, whatever extract he read.

The "New Hobbit"

Tolkien's piece was of great importance in itself as marking a resurgence in his writing of *The Lord of the Rings*. For a while the work had stalled, and notes that Tolkien made on the work during that past summer revealed painful indecision, doubt and a failure of confidence over the direction of the book. His work had in fact faltered over many months during 1939.[7] This coincided with a lengthy period in which he was unwell, including an injury to a leg while gardening.

While it is impossible to tell exactly what extract Tolkien read from the "new Hobbit," as Lewis called it, it must have been from what Christopher Tolkien described as the "third phase" of the story. It is likely to be either the chapter "Ancient History," concerning Gandalf's recent discoveries about the sinister meaning of the Ring of power, or the account of the meeting of the Council in Rivendell that makes up the chapter "In the House of Elrond." The former is most likely, I think.

Both concern the Ring, and spill light on the emerging character of Aragorn (who is still then called Trotter and remains a hobbit rather than a man of lost Númenor). It is clear in this sequence that the Ring is now much more sinister than in earlier drafts and embodies Tolkien's characteristic theme of power and domination much more strongly. Both the relevance and applicability to world events of the time are more present. The Ring, made with Sauron's technological craft, embodied a "hideous strength."[8] Sauron's power was somehow embedded in it, making the Ring an object in which evil was externalized. Not only this, but the Ring of power controlled to varying degrees the other magic rings if used by elves, dwarves and human beings. Indeed, the nine rings and the men who held them had returned to Sauron. In Tolkien's redrafting, as he discovered more and more of the potency of the Ring that had come, not by accident, into Bilbo's hands, he succeeded in portraying evil in such a way that it was applicable to its particular modern manifestation in the current war, including the conflict's reliance on what Churchill called "the lights of perverted science."

Charles Williams's Allegory

Charles Williams's offering to the noisy evening was a short Christmas play, *The House by the Stable*. He had completed this just a few days before. In it, Pride, in the form of a pretty woman, and Hell, her brother, seek to steal the soul (a precious jewel) from man's breast. The devilry is interrupted by the figures of Joseph and the pregnant Mary, who are seeking shelter for the night.

The perverse perspective that marks all wickedness is clear from the beginning of the play. Pride, for Williams, lay at the heart of sin, and drove it. Here Pride seductively says to Man (representing all human beings):

> You are Man, the lord of this great house Earth,
> Or (as its name is called in my country) Sin;
> You are its god and mine; since you first smiled
> And stretched your hand to me and brought me in,
> Since our tenderness began, I have loved you, Man,
> And will—do not doubt; kiss me again.

Man responds in adoring words, remarking at her "dove's eyes" and how she prevents him feeling alone in his "greatness." Pride then says,

> So this wonderful house where moon and sun
> Run with lights, and all kinds of creatures crawl
> To be your servants, and your only business is to take
> Delight in your own might—it is yours and mine,
> A shrine for your godhead, and for me because I am yours.[9]

In focusing on Pride and Hell, and the battle for Man's very soul, Williams, like Tolkien, works a traditional Augustinian view of evil as perversion of good, not something self-existent, into a contemporary form. They, like C. S. Lewis, were very familiar with Augustine's early Christian writings, which so shaped medieval thought. In portraying Man's love as Pride, Williams is not saying that love itself is an evil but that Pride is a distorting of something good. Williams here is not as successful I think as Tolkien in grappling with evil in contemporary form, even though pride is with us always, of course, and was certainly present in and motivating the leaders of the Third Reich. His picture of Man's soul as a lost jewel, however, does have a simple beauty. Williams is more successful in portraying evil in modern form in some of his novels, such as *All Hallows Eve*, which was written later in the war and had a World War II setting.

What is remarkable is the impact of Williams on Lewis, an influence that continued long after he died. By the summer of the next year, after hearing Williams read this play (which would have linked in Lewis's mind with Milton's exploration of pride in *Paradise Lost*) he had had the idea for *The Screwtape Letters*. He took up the rich possibilities of the inverse perspective of hell much further than Williams had. While the play may not have had a direct part in the birth of Screwtape, its reading would have reinforced what Owen Barfield called the *Weltanschauung* or worldview that he felt was part of at least those who were at the center of the Inklings.[10]

A Chapter from *The Problem of Pain*

We do not know which chapter of *The Problem of Pain* Lewis read to the group. Almost any chapter, however, is relevant to the theme that seemed so dominant that evening, and which was remarked on in Lewis's report to his brother in the letter. In the book Lewis defended the view of evil he shared with Tolkien and Williams—the orthodox Christian view that was common to Augustine, Milton, other Inklings like Nevill Coghill and Lewis's brother, and to the Christian creeds. He did this in powerful rhetoric that not only replayed the central philosophical arguments but pulled in a dazzling array of insights from Kenneth Grahame's *The Wind in the Willows*, a German theologian's *The Idea of the Holy* (Rudolf Otto), on the meaning of the sacred as the Other, and speculation about the misuse of artifacts (and, effectively, the machine and technology) in modern manifestations of evil. *The Problem of Pain* also reveals Lewis's position on evil when he was an atheist, and why he found such a position untenable later. The book spans heaven and hell.

In what is a small book Lewis ranges far and wide in his speculations, which include the differences between human and animal consciousness, yet never loses the tight thread of his argument. As Lewis began writing *The Problem of Pain* in the summer of 1939, and read it in installments to the Inklings (to whom it is dedicated), probably from the beginning of term in October, suggests that the chapter read on November 9 was from early in the book. He completed the writing by spring 1940, not long before conceiving *The Screwtape Letters.*

It perhaps was about this time that, having listened to a reading from *The Problem of Pain,* Charles Williams commented that God had not been angry over the complaints of Job in the Bible. Lewis remembered him adding,

> The weight of the divine displeasure had been reserved for the "comforters," the self-appointed advocates on God's side, the people who tried to show that all was well—"the sort of people," he said, immeasurably dropping his lower jaw and fixing me with his eyes—"the sort of people who wrote books on the Problem of Pain."[11]

Lewis characteristically wrote elsewhere about a constant human struggle to reconcile the abstract generalization and the particular instance. The experience of pain in contrast to the concept of pain is one example he gave. He ended by referring humorously to his own book on pain to illustrate the dilemma:

> Human intellect is incurably abstract. Pure mathematics is the type of successful thought. Yet the only realities we experience are concrete—this pain, this pleasure, this dog, this man. While we are loving the man, bearing the pain, enjoying the pleasure, we are not intellectually apprehending Pleasure, Pain or Personality. When we begin to do so, on the other hand, the concrete realities sink to the level of mere instances or examples: we are no longer dealing with them, but with that which they exemplify. . . . As thinkers we are cut off from what we think about; as tasting, touching, willing, loving, hating, we do not clearly understand. . . . You cannot study Pleasure in the

moment of the nuptial embrace, nor repentance while re-penting, nor analyse the nature of humour while roaring with laughter. But when else can you really know these things? "If only my toothache would stop, I could write another chapter about Pain." But once it stops, what do I know about pain?[12]

That evening in November, Lewis's chapter from *The Problem of Pain* was part of a theoretical treatise on evil and suffering, though its application was immediate in the heightened context of war. Tolkien's and Williams's contributions to that meeting had been fiction and poetic drama. Perhaps the group on that occasion (but certainly other times) chewed over the fact that within poetry and within a story and even within history the abstract and the concrete dilemma could be at least partly resolved in, as it were, a "little incarnation," as Lewis once put it, that anticipated or echoed the time when myth became fact in the Gospels. Tolkien had given the Andrew Lang Lecture touching on this very subject earlier that year, March 8, 1939, at St. Andrews University.

Suffering, Evil and a Purgatorial Theme

The likely theme of that evening, which Lewis does not name but instances in the three readings, was one that recurred often throughout wartime meetings, so far as we can tell.

One example of when Tolkien intensified the atmosphere for the Inklings in wartime was his short piece "Leaf by Niggle," written perhaps around April 1942, which he read to his friends. Tolkien was haunted by his task of writing the "new Hobbit" and the larger, un-finished *Silmarillion*. Likewise, "Leaf by Niggle" concerns the di-lemma of Niggle the painter's unfinished work. For Tolkien, a central theme of *The Lord of the Rings* was death,[13] and in "Leaf by Niggle," Niggle's journey can be taken to be an exploration of death and pur-gatory, in which the soul is made ready for heaven. In fact, he referred to it in a letter as "my 'purgatorial' story" which made "visible and physical the effects of Sin or misused Free Will by men."[14] For Sebastian D. G. Knowles, in his study *A Purgatorial Flame*, purgatory is a deep and persistent theme of Tolkien and his Inklings friends, and one which marked other writers in wartime such as T. S. Eliot, W. H. Auden and Evelyn Waugh. A marked influence on these writers was Dante's *Purgatorio*. In the context of the Second World War, he argues, Dante was extraordinarily relevant. Knowles writes,

> One group of [wartime] writers, in particular, makes a concerted and apparently deliberate return to the metaphor [of purgatory]: the Inklings—Charles Williams, C. S. Lewis, and J. R. R. Tolkien. Tolkien writes of a Middle Earth throughout the war, but leaving *The Lord of the Rings* . . . aside, his most unambiguous recreation of purgatory is the lovely allegorical fable, "Leaf By Niggle."[15]

The Charles Williams Factor

Charles Williams read regularly to the Inklings, including extracts from his Arthurian cycle of poetry, probably parts of a novel he abandoned and his final novel, *All Hallows Eve*. The latter is set in wartime London. Characteristically for Williams, two of the protagonists are killed before the novel opens. In the words of the poet and novelist John Wain, who was a young member of the Inklings in the period immediately after the war, Charles Williams "gave himself to Oxford as unreservedly as Oxford gave itself to him." When Tolkien and Lewis arranged for him to teach in the university on Milton and other topics, his lectures were enormously popular. Wain tells how they "were crowded out. . . . Williams, on the platform, enjoyed himself so much that even the most obstinate sceptics in the audience finally capitulated and shared his enjoyment. Great poetry was something to be revelled in, to be rejoiced over, and Williams revelled and rejoiced up there before our eyes."[16]

Charles Williams illustrates how complex the arrangements of the Inklings were in their deliberate lack of instituted formality. He was regular in his attendance at what he sometimes called "the Magdalen set" for the Thursday or sometimes Friday evenings. He also, however, often met just with Lewis, or with only Lewis and Tolkien, or sometimes even with Lewis's brother Warnie alone. I particularly like Lewis's description of an occasion when Williams read to Tolkien and himself from a study of Arthurian legend which was to be curtailed by his sudden death. The reading took place in Lewis's college rooms, where the Inklings so often met for the evening reading sessions.

> Picture to yourself . . . an upstairs sitting-room with windows looking north into the "grove" of Magdalen College on a sunshiny Monday Morning in vacation at about ten o'clock. The Professor and I, both on the Chesterfield, lit our pipes and stretched out our legs. Williams in the arm-chair opposite to us threw his cigarette into the grate, took up a pile of the extremely small, loose sheets on which he habitually wrote—they came, I think, from a twopenny pad for memoranda, and began [reading].[17]

John Wain vividly recalls this period of the Inklings and the meetings in that same room in which Lewis described Williams reading about King Arthur:

> I can see that room so clearly now, the electric fire pumping heat into the dank air, the faded screen that broke some of the keener draughts, the enamel beerjug on the table, the well-worn sofa and armchairs, and the men drifting in (those from distant colleges would be later), leaving overcoats and hats in any corner and coming over to warm their hands before finding a chair. There was no fixed etiquette, but the rudimentary honours

would be done partly by Lewis and partly by his brother, W. H. Lewis, a man who stays in my memory as the most courteous I have ever met—not with mere politeness, but with a genial, self-forgetting considerateness that was as instinctive to him as breathing. Sometimes, when the less vital members of the circle were in a big majority, the evening would fall flat; but the best of them were as good as anything I shall live to see.[18]

C. S. Lewis needed a group of likeminded friends around him. In those wartime years it was the perfect place for him, as well as for Tolkien and Charles Williams, to explore devilry and connected themes. The Inklings listened, sometimes with laughter, to readings from *The Screwtape Letters*, the "new Hobbit," *All Hallows Eve*, *The Great Divorce* and other pieces featuring diabolical goings on, the light of heaven, the shadow of hell and purgatorial suffering.

The Inklings group had an edge to it in that most who attended at that wartime time had experienced combat in World War I. Lewis was typical, in that several of the Inklings had been wounded, such as H. V. D. Dyson (the latter so severely that he had an out-of-the-body experience during the Battle of Passchendaele). When Dyson years later appeared as an elderly literary critic in the movie *Darling*, he walked with a stick, though perhaps this marked the onset of arthritis!

Though there was joking, stories and deep laughter, the underlying content of the Inklings meetings was momentous. Dr. "Humphrey" Havard remembered that, amid laughter, gossip and drinks, *The Screwtape Letters* was read: "It was in this way that the early *Screwtape Letters* first saw daylight. They were greeted hilariously. We heard several of Lewis's poems . . . and chapters from the *Problem of Pain* and *Miracles*."[19]

Dr. Havard portrays the group as having a literary purpose. Lewis and Tolkien also both wrote of the Inklings as a literary club. In the earliest description that names the group, in 1936, Lewis points out that one element the Inklings had in common was a Christian faith. He therefore clearly felt that one enjoyable quality of the club was its shared faith. Lewis and at least some others, so far as he was concerned, stood against the modern world in respect of its unbelieving character. The beliefs that lay at the foundation of societies and cultures were taken with utter seriousness by the leading members of the Inklings, like Tolkien, Lewis, Williams and Barfield. The very friendship and fellowship that Lewis perceived as holding together the group was likely enough, for him, a vestige of an older, fast disappearing world. These principles helped to sustain him as he tried to champion good in a period of war that reflected the larger conflict of good and evil.[20]

The war years gradually opened up to hope of an ending. The Inklings started to plan a victory vacation. Then, at last, Hitler was no more and Germany surrendered soon after. The excitement when Victory in Europe was celebrated resounded around Oxford. In the evening, one of those who walked around looking at the bonfires was Charles Williams, who had spent the day working. The next day, he was gripped by pain and eventually taken to hospital. After surgery he died on May 15, 1945. Lewis discovered the shocking news when he visited the hospital to see his friend, and walked down to the Eagle and Child, a pub, where the Inklings were gathering for their Tuesday morning meeting, to tell them their friend had gone. They knew that the Inklings could never be the same again.

The Inklings and Victory

Though war with Germany ended in May 1945, it was not until August that Japan surrendered, soon after the destruction of Hiroshima and Nagasaki. At the two cities a brief manmade light eclipsed the bright sunlight, bringing instant extinction or a slow death from radiation. Birds burst into flame in midflight. It seemed like the gates of hell had twice opened, briefly casting their deadly fire. The fear of nuclear war had arrived to haunt the human race.

At the end of 1945 those of the friends who could gathered and celebrated a "Victory Inklings." They made themselves at home in a pub called "The Bull" at Fairford, in the Cotswold hills of Gloucestershire, one of Lewis's favorite regions. The celebration lasted four days in December, and the party included Lewis and his brother Warren, Tolkien and, some of the time, Dr. Havard. The depleted group made the best of the "jaunt." The first day Warren Lewis spent walking with Tolkien before the others arrived. Warren recorded events in his diary, including the walks, conversation, quiet reading and moments touched by another world. They were able to dream of the future, which seemed much more hopeful in the joyful absence of world war. He noted late one evening,

> On Thursday . . . [i]n the afternoon we walked through Horcott and Whelford . . . Whelford, a mere Hamlet, has a simple little Church where we all felt that God dwells; nothing to "see" in it. There, to my surprise and pleasure, Tollers said a prayer. Down on the river was a perfect mill house where we amused ourselves by dreaming of it as a home for the Inklings.[21]

The postwar period would see the publication of The Chronicles of Narnia (1950–1956) and The Lord of the Rings (1954–1955). The "new Hobbit" was essentially finished by 1949, though there was much refining to do before Tolkien could be satisfied with the work. Others, inspired by Inklings members, would write books that carried on the vision of the Inklings, such as Roger Lancelyn Green and Harry Blamires. The latter was an important lay theologian, carrying on the tradition of Lewis, Dorothy L. Sayers, G. K. Chesterton and others. Lewis and Tolkien's mature writings of Narnia and Middle-earth either originated in or were mostly written within a period of war or impending war. In them the theme of devilry so central to both writers was particularly successful.

Images of the Dark Side

The Lord of the Rings

I t was no secret that J. R. R. Tolkien did not approve of his friend C. S. Lewis writing theology for the general public. He felt that only those with training in theology should attempt such a task. He was not pleased therefore when Lewis dedicated *The Screwtape Letters* to him. Seen from Lewis's point of view, however, the dedication is less surprising when the extent of devilry is explored in Tolkien's fiction. As well as grand Satan figures—Morgoth and his lieutenant Sauron—his tales abound with images of evil.

These images give a vivid and concrete expression to the age-old discussion of devilry and of the forces of good and evil. In their own way, and drawing on a long tradition of storytelling, Tolkien's widely known images in fact offer a deeply thought out take on the traditional understanding of evil as privation, perversion and parasite. It was this traditional understanding that he shared with C. S. Lewis. Evil is not something that exists independently or has always and inevitably existed, and will exist for ever. Or is it? Did Tolkien fully share Lewis's traditional view?

There is an ongoing debate about the nature of evil in Tolkien. Is it dualistic—representing a battle between good and evil that has been going as long as the universe has been here, or even before—or, like in Lewis, is evil a perversion of good, having no substance of its own and therefore, on the great scale of things, short lived?

The Lord of the Rings, Tom Shippey points out, tries to reconcile two views of evil, the Manichaeist (a dualist view, where good and evil are both primal forces) and the Christian (represented by St. Augustine and Boethius). Both Augustine and Boethius, who were widely read in the Middle Ages and enormously influential, were well-known to both Lewis and Tolkien. One view of evil Shippey calls a "subjective" view and the other "objective."[1] The Augustinian view can be called "subjective" in the sense that evil is entirely negative—it is a perversion or violation of something originally good. It lacks any reality on its own; its existence is owed entirely to the good it is defacing. For Augustine, all God's creation was pronounced by him to be good. In the "objective" view, evil exists in its own nature, rather than only having a derivative, one might say wraithlike, existence.[2]

Professor Shippey is not saying, I think, that evil cannot be objectified, so that an "other" to a person can be created, perhaps as a form of demonic possession or an object endowed with powers. In C. S. Lewis's science-fiction story *Perelandra*, the scientist Edward Weston, who believes that things are only what they are made of, eventually becomes nothing more than an "Un-man," as we shall see in chapter six. Evil has been objectified in his body to the extent that the real Weston has almost disappeared. Many stories of the supernatural have a doppelgänger, or double, and there is something of this in the two warring sides of Gollum—who still carries traces of his hobbit nature—in *The Lord of the Rings*.

In the orthodox Christian view—well represented by St. Augustine—the object that has become bad remains defined only by what it is not. If you had a bowl that was ideal for placing fruit in—a fruit bowl—and you dropped it so that it smashed, it would no longer be a fruit bowl. You could say it had been a fruit bowl, but

not that it is now, because it could no longer function as a recep-
tacle for fruit. You could also say that it is a broken bowl. It has lost
the quality which made it a bowl. In terms of good and evil, you
could say that a bad person is a person who is going bad, who may
yet be healed and restored.

Tolkien, Shippey believes, tries to take account of both sides, the
subjective and the objective, each of which is true to our experience.
He sees this happening with the symbol of the Ring borne by Frodo.
As an evil, it is an objective reality, the power of which is to be re-
sisted. It also however appeals subjectively to a person's weakness.
For instance, the Ring appeals to "possessiveness in Bilbo, fear in
Frodo, patriotism in Boromir, pity in Gandalf."[3]

But does Tolkien's portrayal of the objective reality of evil through
the Ring really reflect a dualistic view of reality? A dualistic view sees
evil as part of the very nature of the universe. Tolkien's Ring, however,
is not the creation of Ilúvatar, the creator of all, but of a creature,
Sauron, a Maia or lesser angelic being who has become depraved.
Even though evil is objectified in the Ring, the description of Manichaeist thought might, in fact, seem truer of Tolkien's myth of the
cosmos: the fall of Melkor, or Morgoth, takes place before the creation
of the world. In his music of creation, on which the making of the
world was to be founded, Ilúvatar incorporates the discord of evil as
a lesser theme, ultimately overcome in the procession of the music—
all this before the beginning of the world. This appears to show a lack
of reconciliation of good and evil in Tolkien's imagination. Such a lack
might seem to suggest Manichaeism, an eternal dualism in the universe. The whole beautiful myth of the creation music of the "Ainu-
lindalë," however, actually rejects a dualism of good and evil. The
discord brought by Melkor is eventually overcome in the music, revealing that it is temporary rather than eternal in the scheme of things.
A greater problem, philosophically and theologically, seems at first
sight to be the existence of the Valar before the beginning of Middle-

earth. This appears to conflict with Tolkien's depiction of the Valar as angels, servants and creations of Ilúvatar, rather than as deities. This apparent contradiction, however, can be reconciled by seeing the world, Eä, within which is Middle-earth, as only part of creation, the larger reality of which includes the created beings of the Valar.

Tolkien is not a dualist in his portrayal of good and evil.[4] In achieving a realistic tension between subjective evil and objectified or external evil, Tolkien's fertile imagination creates many embodiments of evil—Balrogs, dragons, Orcs, the fallen Valar, Morgoth and his servant Sauron, the Ringwraiths, monstrous spiders such as Shelob or Ungoliant, werewolves and trolls. The tension liberated his imagination. There are many cases where a train of reasoning leads to baffling paradoxes or seeming contradictions, while the imagination is able to handle them harmoniously.

In his epic poem *Paradise Lost*, John Milton has often been charged with unwittingly making Satan the hero of his poem, most recently by Philip Pullman, who is glad to acknowledge his debt to Milton in the conception of *His Dark Materials*. To fallen human beings, evil is fatally attractive, and bad characters notoriously are easier to create in fiction than good. Are evil beings such as Morgoth, Sauron or Saruman, and Elves and Men who fall into evil like Fëanor and Denethor, more convincing than Gandalf, Aragorn, Frodo, Beren, or Galadriel? Tolkien however ably creates good beings as well as evil. We are delighted by the vision of Valinor, the earlier days of Númenor, or Rivendell, and the goodness of a Lúthien, Aragorn or Frodo. We understand the tragedy of a Fëanor, Túrin or Boromir.

Set against evil in Tolkien's world are many elements, but rarely physical force (as in the overthrow of Morgoth at the end of the First Age, the destruction of Númenor or Gandalf's fight with the Balrog). Even when the Host of the West assembles before the Black Gate of Mordor in *The Lord of Rings* it is with no hope of military success. One important element countering evil that is central to

Tolkien's world is healing, which is a quality of special places (such as Rivendell and Lórien), of some objects (such as particular plants) and of certain gifted people. A principal healer in *The Lord of Rings* is Aragorn, whose power of healing is part of his true kingship. One of his ancient names was "the Renewer." His healing hands, which echo Christ's, are laid on Faramir, the Lady Éowyn and the Hobbit Merry. There are other counter elements to the powers of evil, including sacrifice of one's life for others. Underlying them all is faith in providence—hope in the ultimate happy ending, held even by people who know they shall not live to see it.

Much of Tolkien's invented mythology concerns creativity and art as a force of good, particularly as the foundation of culture and history. The making of the world by the demiurgic Valar, the fashioning of the Silmarils and the forging of the Rings shape all events in Middle-earth. For Tolkien a study of the powers of evil necessarily has to do with the misuse of creativity and free will. Because of his theology of Middle-earth, Tolkien portrayed evil as utterly real, without falling into a dualism of good and evil. The many occasions of tragedy within his tales (preeminently in the story of Túrin in *The Children of Húrin*) emphasizes the reality of evil powers in the world, evil originated by the fall of Melkor (aka Morgoth). Evil is only possible to creatures capable of creativity and free will. The Orcs, to the contrary, seem to be programmed to inflict evil, acting as tools rather than free agents of Morgoth and Sauron, existing rather like intelligent biological robots. Their actions appear to be their makers' responsibility, not theirs.[5]

Both salvation and damnation in Tolkien's world involve moral choices. Thus evil is indivisible: its implications are applicable to the real world, as well as to Tolkien's invented, secondary world. He would no doubt have approved of what George MacDonald, the nineteenth-century fantasist, wrote: "The laws of the spirit of man must hold, alike in this world and in any world he may invent. . . . In physical things a man may invent: in moral things he must obey—

and take their laws with him into his invented world as well."[6]

It is clear that C. S. Lewis wholeheartedly endorsed Tolkien's view of the moral responsibility involved in human freedom. Lewis's exploration of evil spans his fiction and nonfictional writings. His postwar science fiction story *That Hideous Strength* (1945), which we shall look at in chapter six, has a striking affinity with Tolkien's *The Lord of the Rings* (published 1954–1955). They were both composed in the war years (Lewis's totally and Tolkien's partly) and try to come to terms with an almost unthinkable evil. *That Hideous Strength* gives fictional expression to ethical themes explored in *The Abolition of Man*, a philosophical essay that sees human beings in a post-Christian world, cast adrift from the values that make and sustain our humanity. The late David Porter wrote about how Charles Williams shared many of the concerns of others in the Inklings, particularly those of Tolkien and Lewis.

> In his [Williams's] work evil is often shown as an offence against order: thus in the Arthurian poems the kingdom begins to be weakened. . . . Sin . . . is greed in what should be an exchange of love. Often evil is pictured as an inversion of something that has already been shown to us as an image of the good, or which is good in itself; several evil characters in the novels . . . are counterfeits, mimicking the acts of charity and grace. . . . In *The Descent of the Dove* evil is structural; heaven is a place of mutuality, Hell a place of selfishness. . . . Just as, in *Descent into Hell*, Wentworth's damnation came by tiny sins rather than by huge outrage, so the aberration of Hell needs only minor flaws to show itself: "Hell is always inaccurate," wrote Williams.[7]

A Debt to the Past

Both C. S. Lewis and his friend Tolkien were scholars whose main area of interest was the medieval period. Both, as pointed out before, were very familiar with the early church writings of St. Augustine, whose works were a prime shaper of medieval thought. Not surprisingly, considering Lewis's and Tolkien's debt to this period, St. Augustine's enormously influential Christian view of the nature of evil is strikingly similar to theirs, as we have seen. Because of his historical importance and affinity with these writers, I'll briefly mention his central idea about the nature of evil.

Augustine's view is expounded in his autobiographical *Confessions* (written A.D. 397). At one point in his account Augustine looked back to his thirty-first year. He realized then that the cause of sin lies in the wrong exercise of free will, and went on to reject the Manichaean heresy, with its eternal dualism of good and evil. Though he had abandoned belief in astrology by that time, he was perplexed and miserable about the origin of evil. He had found in the Platonists the seeds of the doctrine of the divinity of the Word, but not of his incarnation. Finally he discovered the truth about Christ through the study of Scripture, especially St. Paul's letters. He saw that it follows from the incarnation—God taking on the real flesh of a human being—that the world and humanity is in its created nature good, and that the evil is only in evidence as a corruption of what is good. As existence itself is a good, evil cannot exist of itself; it has no substance.

> It was manifested unto me, that those things be good which yet are corrupted. . . . So long therefore as they are, they are good: therefore whatsoever is, is good. That evil then which I sought, whence it is, is not any substance: for were it a substance, it should be good. For either it should be an incorruptible substance, and so a chief good: or a corruptible substance; which unless it were good, could not be corrupted. I perceived therefore, and it was manifested to me that Thou madest all things good, nor is there any substance at all, which Thou madest not; and for that Thou madest not all things

equal, therefore are all things; because each is good, and altogether very good, because our God made all things very good.

And to Thee is nothing whatsoever evil: yea, not only to Thee, but also to Thy creation as a whole, because there is nothing without, which may break in, and corrupt that order which Thou hast appointed it. . . .

And I enquired what iniquity was, and found it to be no substance, but the perversion of the will, turned aside from Thee, O God, the Supreme.[8]

Evil understood as corruption and perversion of good is exactly how evil is represented in *The Lord of the Rings* and The Chronicles of Narnia.

Cosmic Battle

We have seen how C. S. Lewis tends to picture the human struggle between tendencies to good and evil in terms of a cosmic battle, but not an eternal one. The same is true of Tolkien. To see this, let's look a little more closely at the background to Lewis's thinking about this. The two friends had a vision of goodness that is expressed in order, harmony and an organic rather than mechanistic view of nature. Lewis found some of this ideal captured in the dominant worldview of the sixteenth century—one of alchemy and high magic. Lewis saw that century still steeped in a perception of the world it had inherited from the vast medieval period.

In his Oxford history, *English Literature in the Sixteenth Century*, Lewis paints a memorable picture of this old white or "high" magic, which he sharply distinguishes from satanic or dark magic. In the sixteenth century, observes Lewis, there was an "animistic or genial cosmology," where nature was perceived as "a festival not a machine." It was not until toward the end of that century that the beginnings of the scientific movement "delivered nature into our hands." This increasingly mechanistic perception of nature, in contrast to a cosmos full of life, affected both thought and emotion—it lost an essential harmony and wholeness. Lewis argues,

> By reducing Nature to her mathematical elements it substituted a mechanical for a genial or animistic conception of the universe. The world was emptied, first of her indwelling spirits, then of her occult sympathies and antipathies, finally of her colours, smells, and tastes. . . . The result was dualism rather than materialism. The mind, on whose ideal constructions the whole method depended, stood over against its object in ever sharper dissimilarity. Man with his new powers became rich like Midas but all that he touched had gone dead and cold. This process, slowly working, ensured during the next century the loss of the old mythological imagination: the conceit, and later the personified abstraction, takes its place. Later still, as a desperate attempt to bridge a gulf which begins to be found intolerable, we have the Nature poetry of the Romantics.[9]

If Lewis is right, we in the modem world have inherited this dualism of a mechanized view of nature, leaving us with the dilemma of how to re-enchant the world. In his inaugural lecture, when taking up the Chair of Medieval and Renaissance Literature in Cambridge in 1954, Lewis spoke of the contrast between this harmonious view and that of the contemporary world.[10] He described the present time as the Age of the Machine—on the large pattern of the Stone Age, the Bronze Age and similar.

Tolkien elaborated essentially the same view in his themes of power and possession, central to his fiction. The wrong use of power is often expressed in Tolkien in magic, the mechanical and the technological. His Dark Lords Morgoth and Sauron, and the bent wizard Saruman, experiment with genetic engineering and use or encourage the use of machines in order to enslave free peoples. Sauron, in fact, is the supreme technocrat: the Ring itself is a product of his technological skill, in which he stores part of himself (rather like Voldemort and his Horcruxes that play such an important part in the Harry Potter stories). Tolkien distinguishes art from this kind of magic, art which is typified in the Elves, who have no desire for possession. Tolkien, like Lewis, saw a machine attitude, or what might be called technocracy, as the modern form of magic, seeking to enslave and possess nature, rather than to steward her. He may have discussed with his friend the view that in the modern world the human being is seen only as part of nature; humans are therefore equally fair game for such control and possession by a powerful few.

The magical power of modem technocracy—the instinct to possess at any cost—is not for Tolkien necessarily the same as domination or rule, which he sees as not wholly bad. Domination, in fact, is meant to be a form of stewardship. Denethor of Gondor and Gandalf can be contrasted as bad and good stewards, as they exercise responsibility over others. Tom Bombadil is also a good model of stewardship; he is guardian of the Old Forest who has no desire to possess, and who is thereby invulnerable to the desire of the Ring. The earlier Ages of Middle-earth are dominated by Elves, who nevertheless avoided possession as usurpation. The dominance of humankind in the Fourth Age of Middle-earth (the period in which *The Lord of the Rings* is set) is meant to be modeled on Elven values, not to be a destructive territorial rivalry. The stories set in the earlier ages of Middle-earth are to be found in *The Silmarillion*, and many volumes of unfinished material such as *The History of Middle-earth* (12 vols.).

The theme of possession is focused by the two central motifs of Tolkien's stories of Middle-earth, the Silmarils (beautiful gems that carry the original light of the world) and the Ring. The Silmarils are wholly good, and the Ring is wholly evil, yet each test those who come into contact with them. King Thingol, father of Lúthien, tragically falls morally in desiring a Silmaril; Beren has no desire to possess it. Rather he loves the greater treasure, Lúthien the Elven princess, who is better than any possession. Boromir of Gondor succumbs to the desire of the Ring; Bilbo resists it, as does Galadriel; it has little power over the humble Sam.

In chapter seven we shall consider Lewis's symbolic map of the world in his *The Pilgrim's Regress*, which is a master key to the story in its depiction of dangers to the north and south. Lewis repeated this *mappa mundi* to some extent in Narnian geography, in that there are dangers to the humane and balanced kingdom of Narnia from north and south. There is a rather similar symbolic geography in Tolkien, also with dangers from north and south. In the earlier ages of Middle-earth, Angband constituted a particular danger from the north. The dragon Glaurung was another northern threat. In the Third Age, there was Angmar, the Witch-Kingdom, to the north, and Mordor in the opposite direction, and still further to the south, the regions of Harad.

The Dark Lords Morgoth and Sauron, powerful images of the powers of evil, dominate Tolkien's stories as the most powerful dangers facing Middle-earth.

Morgoth. This name, Morgoth ("the black enemy"), was given to the fallen Vala or archangel Melkor after he helped to extinguish the original light of the world from the Two Trees that towered over Middle-earth and had also stolen the ancient gems, the Silmarils.

Morgoth is an equivalent in Tolkien's mythology to the biblical Satan, or Lucifer, who was originally an angel of high rank who rebelled against God. Tolkien highlights the appalling malice of Morgoth, and the effect of this malice on events in Middle-earth's history. Morgoth figures in *The Silmarillion*, being cast out of the world at the end of the First Age. In the Second and Third Ages his less powerful but more subtly evil lieutenant, Sauron, takes his place. In Tolkien's stories, Morgoth became jealous of his maker, Ilúvatar, which led him to seek the secret of the creation principle, rather than merely being an agent and servant of his creator. His rebellion introduced discord into the world.

Morgoth used darkness and cold as a weapon, extinguishing the light of the Two Lamps and using Ungoliant, the monstrous spider, to devour the light of the Two Trees. After seizing the Silmarils, Morgoth returned to the icy northern wastes of Middle-earth, to Angband. Here he planned the subjugation of ancient Beleriand, breeding Orcs and other monsters. One of the greatest deeds of resistance to him was the stealing back of a Silmaril from his Iron Crown by Beren and Lúthien, the lovers who presage the union between the human Aragorn and the Elf Arwen in *The Lord of the Rings*.

Sauron. The greatest of Morgoth's servants, Sauron's deeds encompass three Ages of Middle-earth, until his crushing downfall with the War of the Ring (as told in *The Lord of the Rings*). In origin he is one of the lesser guardians and stewards of creation, of the same order of angelic being as Gandalf the wizard. In Tolkien's *The Silmarillion* he appears in the tale of Beren and Lúthien, figures strongly in the fall of Númenor and clandestinely creates the One Ring to rule the Rings of Power. Though he loses the Ring to the ill-fated Isildur, by near the end of the Third Age he has consolidated his power enough to attempt to subjugate the Middle-earth that remains, as his master, Morgoth, had attempted long before to enslave the now drowned region of Beleriand.

Sauron is a more nuanced image of incarnate evil than Morgoth. Before being caught in the destruction of Númenor, he had been able to assume an attractive appearance, which helped him to win over the minds of Elves and humans. He successfully concealed his lust for power and control. He very nearly succeeded in seducing the Elves of Eregion to the "magic" of technology—what Tolkien called "machinery." In a letter, Tolkien remarked that at "Eregion great work began—and the Elves came their nearest to falling to 'magic' and machinery."[11]

Sauron's great innovation in evil was his creation of the Ring of power, which draws upon a potent motif in traditional storytelling.

The Ring of Sauron. The Ring at the center of Tolkien's famous story is one of the Rings of power that were largely fashioned by Noldorin Elves in Eregion in the Second Age of Middle-earth. They made Three Rings for the Elves, Seven Rings for the Dwarves, and Nine Rings for humankind. In characteristic treachery, Sauron later secretly created the One Ring to rule the others.

Just as the tales of the First Age of Middle-earth are dominated by the motif of the Silmarils, the events of the Third Age, particularly as it reached its climax with the War of the Ring, are dominated by the motif of the Rings.

Gandalf interprets the significance of the Rings, and particularly the ruling Ring, vividly before the final battle against Sauron at the Black Gate of Mordor. The wizard warns the leaders of the armies of the West that they cannot win a final victory over the Dark Lord; such a victory is not to be gained by military might. He tells them that his hope for overcoming the enemy is not in strength of arms, because of the power of the Ring. If it comes again into Sauron's possession their courage and fighting skill will count for nothing. If, however, Frodo and Sam succeed in destroying the Ring, Sauron will lose strength to such an extent that it would be impossible to imagine him ever returning to power. In fact, "all that was made or begun with that power will crumble, and he will be maimed for ever, becoming a mere spirit of malice that gnaws itself in the shadows, but cannot again grow or take shape."[12]

In one of his many letters explaining points in his stories Tolkien comments on Sauron's almost total supremacy in Middle-earth:

> But to achieve this he had been obliged to let a great part of his own inherent power (a frequent and very significant motive in myth and fairy-story) pass into the One Ring. While he wore it, his power on earth was actually enhanced. But

even if he did not wear it, that power existed and was in "rapport" with himself: he was not "diminished."[13]

The One Ring and Voldemort's Horcruxes from the Harry Potter Stories

There are important affinities between Tolkien's Ring and the Horcruxes in the popular Harry Potter stories, owing to both storytellers drawing upon what Tolkien called a "frequent and very significant motive in myth and fairy-story." Rowling's Dark Lord, Voldemort, has a philosophy expressed by one of his faithful servants: "There is no good and evil, there is only power, and those too weak to seek it."[14] Voldemort, unlike Sauron, is human, turning to evil in his youth and seeking immortality. His main strategy is to divide his soul into pieces, embodied in objects called Horcruxes, which include physical things such as a diary, a locket and even other living beings. This allows him to survive, albeit at first in a disembodied state, after his death curse against the baby Harry goes wrong. Harry quickly recognizes Voldemort as the supreme manifestation of evil and as his enemy.

Voldemort's discovery and exploitation of Horcruxes, upon which he misplaces his faith, reveals his character and commitment to great evil. To make a Horcrux the soul has to be sundered, rupturing its original wholeness. The consequence is that, even if a magician's body is destroyed, that person cannot die while the Horcrux remains, for a part of the soul remains embodied in the object. Furthermore, the soul can only be divided as a result of the magician committing murder, which splits the soul, as it is such a gross violation of nature.

George MacDonald was in many ways a forerunner of both Tolkien and Lewis in his concerns, expressed both in fiction and literary essay. In his short story *The Giant's Heart*, a giant's strength is stored in his heart that is hidden apart from his body, his severed heart being rather like the Ring in Tolkien or a Horcrux in Harry Potter. In his essay "On Fairy-Stories," Tolkien illuminates this characteristic motif from myth and fairy tale. This is the notion, he says, "that the life or strength of a man or creature may reside in some other place or thing; or in some part of the body (especially the heart) that can be detached and hidden in a bag, or under a stone, or in an egg."[15] As examples he writes of MacDonald's story as well as a millennia-old Egyptian tale preserved on a papyrus. He quotes from this Egyptian *The Tale of the Two Brothers*, where the younger tells the older brother,

> I shall enchant my heart, and I shall place it upon the top of the flower of the cedar. Now the cedar will be cut down and my heart will fall to the ground, and thou shalt come to seek for it, even though thou pass seven years in seeking it; but when thou has found it, put it into a vase of cold water, and in very truth I shall live.[16]

Charles Williams features this placing of a person's power in an external object. In his last novel, *All Hallows Eve*, he clearly denounces the dark arts of magic. His character representative of supreme evil is Simon the Clerk. Simon has his own quasi-religious order which offers false healing and a perverse group-bond based on insect-like submission. Williams's own ideal of community is what he called in real life the "Order of the Co-inherence," which sees fully human life as based on mutual receiving and giving. This theme dominates his writings. In contrast, like Voldemort with his Horcruxes and Sauron with his ruling Ring, Simon embeds part of his powers in two zombie-like creatures who serve him. The creatures carry "the most secret corridors of his heart." They are in effect clones of Simon the Clerk, crudely realized doppelgangers. Ironically, therefore, the archegoist can be said to die at his own hand when the creatures turn on and destroy him.

The magical plays a great part in the fiction of both Lewis and Tolkien. As mentioned before, they each came to see the modem form of the magical as being technology, which, like all that is magical, can be used or misused, but is particularly susceptible to misuse. In *The Lord of the Rings*, the central image, the Ring, is a kind of ultimate engine or machine into which the Dark Lord has poured his soul. When technology is misused it takes on a life of its own, becoming what the Old Testament prophets called an idol.[17] A whole society can become technocratic, that is, ruled by what might be called a machine mentality. The processes of dehumanization become objective as they are externalized. Such is a society ruled by Sauron and the wizard Saruman; such is a future state of humanity envisioned by the N.I.C.E. in Lewis's *That Hideous Strength*. In *The Screwtape Letters* (as we saw in chap. 2), hell works by efficient bureaucracy, echoing Hitler's Nazi state, which existed even as the Screwtape book was being written, where even the details of victims doomed to perish in the death camps were meticulously recorded.

Light in Tolkien

From looking at images of the dark side in Tolkien it has become clear that, like C. S. Lewis, he had an overriding vision of a cosmos that is full of life, where our tragedy is that we have lost an essential harmony and wholeness in which our humanity can thrive. It is important to see Tolkien's dark images in his wider context of hope. Though his images are fresh and have wide—in fact global—appeal, he intentionally employs what can be called stock images of good and evil taken from fairy story and the rich history of English language and literature. Like Lewis, he was a medieval scholar, and that vast period was a source to him of imaginative nourishment, which lay behind his making of Middle-earth.

C. S. Lewis spoke of the necessity of stock images and the importance of regaining them in art of all kinds:

> It is of the very nature of thought and language to represent
> what is immaterial in picturable terms. What is good or happy
> has always been high like the heavens and bright like the sun.
> Evil and misery were deep and dark from the first. Pain is
> black in Homer, and goodness is a middle point for Alfred no
> less than for Aristotle. To ask how these married pairs of sen-
> sibles and insensibles first came together would be great folly;
> the real question is how they ever came apart, and to answer
> that question is beyond the province of the mere historian.[18]

An image that is the natural opposite of darkness, and the dark side
as representing evil, is of course light. The quality of light is a major
theme in Tolkien's fiction.[19] Even a brief look at the part that light
plays in his narrative helps us to understand how Tolkien captures
the attraction of goodness over evil and portrays the importance of
hope and the longings of the human heart in the ultimate defeat of
wickedness. Light expresses the sovereignty of goodness.

Through Tolkien's tales of Middle-earth he builds up a precise and
careful meaning to light. Rather than a postmodern New Age meaning
or, say, an intellectual concept of humanistic enlightenment, Tolkien's
inspiration and model is biblical, as is so much of English literature. It
could also be called, using Lewis's terminology, "old Western" and also
"pagan" in a sense that both Tolkien and he would apply to the pre-
Christian classical and old northern worlds. A contemporary label
might be that his use of the image of light is premodern.

Verlyn Flieger has made a major study of the relationship of light,
language and biblical content in Tolkien. In *Splintered Light: Logos
and Language in Tolkien's World* (1983) she writes that the Silmarillion

> is a vast, fantasy mythology with the familiar mythological
> themes—gods and men, creation, transgression, love, war,
> heroism, and doom. But more than anything else, and more
> than most mythologies, it is a story about light. Images of light

in all stages—brilliant, dim, whole, refracted—pervade the songs and stories of Tolkien's fictive world, a world peopled by sub-creators whose interactions with the light shape Middle-earth and their own destinies. Tolkien's use of light in The Silmarillion derives from his Christian belief.[20]

Clyde Kilby, who was able to discuss Tolkien's fiction with him, speaks of the contrast of light and darkness always being emphasized in *The Lord of the Rings*. In *Tolkien and the Silmarillion*, Kilby points out some of the many affinities between Tolkien's and the biblical imagination. This affinity is startlingly evident in the case of the creation of light. Like the Bible, in Tolkien light is created before the existence of the sun and moon. The sun and moon are creatures, not deities.

Light itself is associated, Flieger points out, with the divine Logos, the light of the world, Christ himself. We see by him. Light in Tolkien's world is a sign of providence, accomplished by the agency of the Valar, and defiled by the primal enemy of Elven and human life, Melkor (or Morgoth), the equivalent of Lucifer, who became darkened as Satan.

The abiding image of light in Tolkien's world is the Two Trees, extinguished by the visible darkness of Ungoliant, ancestor of the monster spider Shelob encountered by Frodo and Sam as they enter Mordor. Some of the light of the Trees had, however, been captured in the Silmarils, wonderful gems of power fashioned by Fëanor. Fëanor's desire to recover the Silmarils, stolen by Morgoth, is a prime element in the events of the First Age of Middle-earth.

As part of the theme of gradation and splintering of light, Tolkien creates the beautiful period of twilight in Middle-earth before the rising of sun and moon (the time when humans appear). The Elves, created in the twilight, looked upon and saw the dazzling stars. They were called to the light that exists in the Undying Lands of Valinor—

the light of the Two Trees. Consequently, they journeyed in quest of those lands, some unwillingly. Not all complete the journey but remain in Middle-earth, in the twilight. This division affects the history and thus the language of the Elves, Quenya being the language of the Elves of Valinor, and Sindarin, the speech of those remaining in Middle-earth.

Tolkien's portrayal of the twilight is haunted with a sense of the numinous and the presence of Varda. "A Elbereth Gilthoniel" is an Elven hymn or prayer to her. After the rising of the sun and moon, the stars in the night sky continued to comfort and give hope to those faithful to Ilúvatar. The Seven Stars, the Sickle of the Valar, had been placed in the sky by the angelic power of Varda as a sign of the ultimate defeat of Morgoth.

As well as the delicate symbolism of the gradation of light, darkness is a powerful image in Tolkien, again biblical, of all that is the enemy of human life in its full purpose. From the darkness that moved with the arachnid Ungoliant to the blackness of Shelob's Lair, from the burning black of Morgoth's hands by the Silmarils he clutched to the threat of the Black Riders in the long-protected Shire, darkness is present through the tales as a palpable image of evil. Sam in Mordor, well-versed in the history of Middle-earth, was able to see that "in the end the Shadow was only a small and passing thing: there was light and beauty for ever beyond its reach."

A powerful image related to that of light is fire. In *The Silmarillion* we learn that there is a Secret Fire at the heart of real (rather than only envisaged) being. The Secret Fire has its approximate biblical equivalent in the Holy Spirit. Gandalf (who goes in title from "the Grey" to "the White") declares himself the servant of the Secret Fire and bears the Ring of Fire, Narya. The Elf Círdan passed this Ring onto Gandalf when the wizard arrived in Middle-earth: "Take this ring, Master," he said, "for your labours will be heavy; but it will support you in the weariness that you have taken upon yourself. For this is the Ring of Fire, and with it you may rekindle hearts in a world that grows chill."[21]

The Elven prince Fëanor, like Gandalf, is associated with fire. His name, given to him by his mother, is prophetic and means "Spirit of fire." He is the epitome of Elven creativity and craftsmanship. Yet instead of being a servant of the Secret Fire like Gandalf, he desired possession of it, like Morgoth before him. Thus he was unwilling to give back the Silmarils after the destruction of the Two Trees so that their light might be used. His pride in his achievement led him to foolishly pursue Morgoth into Middle-earth, which had far-reaching consequences for the Elves.

The story of Eärendil, the great mariner, displays the theme of light with great power. In Eärendil, the human who became the brightest star in the night sky over Middle-earth, Tolkien succeeded in making a herald of Christ, a prefigurement of the Savior. The light came from the Silmaril on Eärendil's brow, bringing hope to the faithful in the world below.

Right and Wrong as a Clue to Meaning

The Problem of Pain and *Mere Christianity*

In the 1930s, almost right from his conversion to Christianity, C. S. Lewis attempted to communicate Christian faith. He then chose the story form to do this, as we shall see in part two. He soon realized that *The Pilgrim's Regress* had failed to reach a wider readership, even though his publisher had been impressed by it. It was too complex, he concluded, and the meaning wasn't always clear. His next attempt at fiction, *Out of the Silent Planet* (see chap. 6), was far more successful. He was surprised, however, that the strongly Christian elements built into the story usually went unnoticed by reviewers. It made him realize, as he wrote in a letter, that "any amount of theology can now be smuggled into people's minds under cover of romance without their knowing it."[1] This was an important principle he had discovered, which shaped his future works of fiction. It still left unresolved the issue of communicating his faith more overtly and didactically, however.

Wartime Talks on "Mere" Christianity

World War II started the year after the publication of *Out of the Silent Planet*. The war years were to mark his emerging presence as a popular communicator of the Christian faith. He still had much to learn about how to communicate, six years after the appearance of *The Pilgrim's Regress,* and theologians didn't seem to be much use. It was lay Christian writers like G. K. Chesterton, Charles Williams and Dorothy L. Sayers who showed the way. His efforts to communicate faith lucidly and imaginatively were driven by the reality of the war that was raging.

An important step was a book he was asked to write for "The Christian Challenge Series," which was published in 1940 under the title *The Problem of Pain.* It would be his first nonfiction work of Christian apologetics (or defense of the faith). The series' authors were largely, but not entirely, made up of theologians. Its intention was to reach people outside of the church. Lewis's book stood out, even among its more distinguished contributors, in its freshness and range of knowledge. The outstanding Oxford theologian Austin Farrer later commented that Lewis in *The Problem of Pain* presented "a world haunted by the supernatural, a conscience haunted by the moral absolute, a history haunted by the divine claim of Christ."[2] There are many hints of the conversations over the nature of obedience, goodness and evil that would appear in his second science fiction story, *Perelandra* (*Voyage to Venus*), three years later.

For a such a small book, Lewis seemed effortlessly to range far and wide, talking about God's control over all human events—including pain and suffering—the goodness of God and human wickedness, the fall of humankind, animal pain, and hell and heaven. It begins, like his later wartime broadcast talks, on the common ground of ordinary human experience—in this case, very real questions about the all-powerful God's seeming inability to prevent suffering and pain. Charles Williams had heard some of the book read to the Inklings. Reviewing it, he wrote, "Mr Lewis's style . . . is what style always is—goodness working on goodness, a lucid and sincere intellect at work on the facts of life or the great statements of other minds. . . . The chapter on

Animal pain is perhaps especially valuable, as that of hell is especially terrifying, and that on Divine Omnipotence especially lucid."[3]

Williams in his review drew attention to Lewis's chapter on hell; there is a balancing chapter in *The Problem of Pain* on heaven. These chapters relate the existence of hell and heaven to the reality of free will in human beings, yet without trying to satisfy curiosity about factual details of the afterlife. It looks at them as the outcome of moral choices and the sometime reluctant acceptance or willful refusal of salvation. Of hell, Lewis himself says in *The Problem of Pain* that there exists "no doctrine which I would more willingly remove from Christianity than this." The "heaven" chapter is deeply lyrical in places, presenting a longing for God as the deepest desire of the human being, but without sentimentality.

Such was the interest it created that *The Problem of Pain* reprinted after just two months of first publication on October 14, 1940, near the end of the historic Battle of Britain—a turning point in World War II. This publication marked the beginning of the rise of Lewis's popularity as a communicator of Christian belief. It was to lead to an invitation to broadcast on national radio with the BBC. The broadcasts were to boost sales of this book, and his even more popular book, *The Screwtape Letters*, two years later.

The BBC Takes the Initiative

The British Broadcasting Corporation had a strong religious and moral emphasis, heightened by the anxieties and terrors of war experienced by listeners and broadcasters alike. The fledgling TV services were suspended at the beginning of the war, cutting the BBC's lead in the new medium, leaving only the medium of radio and publication of broadcast material in the BBC's weekly magazine, *The Listener*.[4]

The BBC was looking for suitable individuals for broadcast talks that would strengthen and hearten listeners in a way that was necessarily realistic. Many urban listeners were in mortal danger from bombing as London and numerous other large cities such as Portsmouth, Southampton, Coventry and Birmingham were blitzed. Indeed, even Broadcasting House, in central London, didn't escape! Bruce Belfrage was in the process of reading the news in Broadcasting House:

> This is the BBC Home and Forces Programme. Here is the news and this is Bruce Belfrage reading it. Tonight's talk after this bulletin will be by Lord Lloyd the Colonial Secretary. [There follows the sound of a massive explosion lasting around ten seconds before Belfrage continues without any reference at all to the interruption.] The story of recent naval successes in the Mediterranean is told in an Admiralty communication . . .[5]

Seven people in the building were killed and many more were casualties when the 500-pound bomb exploded.

The Reverend James Welch of BBC Religious Broadcasting was on the hunt for people suitable for giving broadcast talks, which might follow a grim news bulletin. His mission for broadcasting was as follows:

> In a time of uncertainty and questioning it is the responsibility of the Church—and of religious broadcasting as one of its most powerful voices—to declare the truth about God and His relation to men. It has to expand the Christian faith in terms that can be easily understood by ordinary men and women, and to examine the ways in which that faith can be applied to present-day society during these difficult times.[6]

Welch discovered someone whom he became convinced would fit the bill. Not a theologian, nor a church minister, but an Oxford don who had written a book on popular theology that gripped him to the core. That book was *The Problem of Pain*. Welch wrote to Lewis inviting him to broadcast and suggesting a couple of ideas for areas he might cover. Lewis wrote back positively and put forward his own idea for a series of talks. He wanted to talk about ideas of right and wrong, and how they gave clues to the meaning of the universe.

It seems to me that the New Testament, by preaching repentance and forgiveness, always *assumes* an audience who already believe in the law of nature and know they have disobeyed it. In modern Britain we cannot at present assume this, and therefore most apologetic begins a stage too far on. The first step is to create, or recover, a sense of guilt. Hence if I gave a series of talks, I shall mention Christianity only at the end, and would prefer not to unmask my battery till then.[7]

The radio talks, which eventually went on into four series over several years (1941, 1942, 1944) were straightforward and lucid, providing an outstanding example of early media evangelism. They survive today in the collection published as *Mere Christianity* (1952), which continues to be an effective presentation of basic Christian belief in the twenty-first century, well over seventy years after the talks were transmitted by the BBC.[8]

James Welch had invited Lewis to give these hugely popular talks early in 1941, when war had already made people generally more thoughtful about ultimate issues. Lewis increasingly regarded England as a post-Christian country. In his view, many people were convinced that they had left Christianity behind, when in fact they had never been true believers in the first place or even had a proper introduction to it. His feelings about the first set of talks were recorded in a letter. The broadcasts, he revealed, were pre-evangelism rather than evangelism—their aim was to persuade modern people that there is a moral law, that we are guilty of disobeying it. The existence of a lawgiver followed very probably, at least, from the reality of the moral law. Unless the Christian doctrine of the atonement (what Christ accomplished in his death and resurrection) was added to this bleak analysis, he concluded, it imparted despair rather than consolation.

Lewis's opening to the series—where he pointed to an objective sense of right and wrong in human moral judgment—was soon expanded into a lecture series published as a philosophical treatise. *The Abolition of Man* (1943) argued that this deeply embedded sense was part of what makes us human. Without it we descend into man's inhumanity to man and the loss of the human.

Lewis's lucid account of the testimony of moral law was in brief fifteen-minute broadcasts. They were made vivid and accessible by his masterly use of images and examples, which is a hallmark of the subsequent talks as well. This concrete and imaginative use of language was intended to aid communication and avoid abstraction. His approach did not go down well with some of his Oxford colleagues, including Tolkien, who felt that teaching about Christianity, even on a popular level, should be left to the theologically trained. Let cobblers stick to their lasts.

While the first series of talks on right and wrong prepared the ground, the next series, "What Christians believe" went right into central issues of good and evil and the presence of devilry in human affairs. Lewis was at pains to point out the limited reach of evil powers in the universe. The first three broadcasts of the new series set the framework for understanding what Christians believe, or "mere Christianity": "The Rival Conceptions of God," "The Invasion," and "The Shocking Alternative."

These chapters set out differences between the main supernatural views of God (found in Judaism, Christianity and Islam) and current rivals—materialism (physical nature is the whole show) and pantheism (everything that exists is somehow divine). The differences include how we see good and evil (pantheism for instance can only see good and evil as the same). Evil in fact is an invasion into a good universe. There are only two views, argues Lewis, which square up to the facts. (1) The view that we live in a good world that has gone wrong. (2) The view that there are two equal and independent powers battling in the universe, one good and one evil, and the battle will never end. The chapter "The Shocking Alternative" points out the importance of free will, which is central to Lewis's case. Without it we would be robots, not capable of loving God and others, or of moral and immoral behavior. It goes on to point out various things God has done to help us, culminating in sending his one and only Son. Lewis's argument is fuller and more subtle and engaging than this brief summary can suggest.

Lewis was joined on the BBC airwaves by his friend and fellow writer Dorothy L. Sayers. (We shall look briefly at her play *The Devil to Pay* in chapter six.) Though Lewis's broadcasts are well known today through their collection in *Mere Christianity*, Sayers's radio drama *The Man Born to Be King*, however, is also important. The episodes were broadcast from December 21, 1941, to October 10, 1942. They dramatized the life of Christ in a down-to-earth, accessible manner, leading of course to their climax in Christ's death for the sake of the world and triumphant resurrection.

During many weeks, therefore, BBC listeners could hear both an episode of *The Man Born to Be King* and a broadcast by Lewis. Both fitted well into the wartime mood, and both were immensely popular. Dorothy L. Sayers's radio drama provoked extremely strong reactions from some Christian leaders, not least because the innovation of hearing an actor, Robert Speaight, giving voice to Christ in colloquial English was shocking and even blasphemous for some. The play's sometimes use of American slang was offensive to some oversensitive English ears. Sayers's attitude was that some religious leaders were so careful to say nothing that would offend that they ended up saying nothing at all! Fortunately, the BBC fully supported her endeavor, being much more in touch with their audience, and with the street language in which the Gospels were written, than those religious leaders.

With Lewis's success in broadcasting Christian belief in a popular manner came a request to give talks to RAF personnel. Lewis gave the talks under his ever-present conviction that an even greater and far more important conflict was raging, the battle for the individual human soul. His very first talk, at RAF Abingdon near Oxford, he considered as nothing short of an abject failure. The experience of speaking to men who had a very realistic view of their unlikelihood of survival brought it home to Lewis how necessary it was to avoid religious jargon, or even precise concepts, honed over a vast period of history, that had become unfamiliar in a post-Christian milieu. Many of those to whom he spoke in this period were unlikely to survive the usual first quota of bombing missions or defensive action against enemy forces.

Humphrey Stuart Babbage, a Royal Air Force chaplain, invited Lewis to speak to a bomber squadron in Norfolk. "Our casualties," he remembered,

> had been heavy: we were, at the time, engaged in massive night bombings against some of the most heavily fortified targets in Germany and occupied Europe. A tour of duty consisted of thirty or more operations against enemy targets: after that, a man was taken off for a period of rest before being scheduled for another tour. The grim fact was that, on the average, a man only completed thirteen raids before being killed or posted missing. These men (in the glory of their budding manhood) knew, statistically speaking, that there was little chance of their completing even one tour.[9]

Lewis's experiences with the RAF led him to work very hard to be more successful in his speaking to nonacademic people. Despite his heavy academic workload, writing projects and visits to RAF airfields, Lewis also found time to engage with his peers who did not accept his faith. Less than two years into the war Oxford University Socratic Club was set up by a parish worker to university women students, Stella Aldwinckle. Its purpose was to discuss questions about Christian faith raised by atheists, agnostics and those disillusioned about religion. Lewis accepted her invitation to be its first president, a position he held until the end of 1954, when he went to Cambridge University to teach.

The club's committee scoured the pages of *Who's Who*, which listed eminent Britons and was published annually, to find notable atheists or other contemporary thinkers who had the time or the zeal to come and present their positions. Leading Christian thinkers also were main speakers. As president, Lewis usually was expected to provide a rejoinder to lead speakers. They included many distinguished philosophers or leading scientists of the time, such as C. E. M. Joad, Peter Medawar, H. H. Price, C. H. Waddington, A. J. Ayer, J. D. Bernal, Antony Flew, Jacob Bronowski, Basil Mitchell, R. M. Hare, Gilbert Ryle, Michael Polanyi and Michael Dummett. Other speakers included Lewis's friends Charles Williams, Dr. "Humphrey" Havard, Austin Farrer and Dorothy L. Sayers. A leading philosopher and fellow Christian, G. E. M. Anscombe, challenged one of Lewis's central arguments against naturalism (that is, against the materialist view that nature is all that is). Lewis reasoned that believing nature is all that is undermined thought itself and was thus self-refuting. Anscombe forced him to clarify and rework his argument, which she did however believe to have considerable merit. Lewis's rather subtle argument takes up a basic point wittily summarized by J. B. S. Haldane and quoted by Lewis:

> It seems to me immensely unlikely that mind is a mere by-product of matter. For if my mental processes are determined wholly by the motions of atoms in my brain I have no reason to suppose that my beliefs are true. They may be sound chemically, but that does not make them sound logically. And hence I have no reason for supposing my brain to be composed of atoms.[10]

Though Lewis was in his element as a traditional philosopher concerned with big questions, encounters such as those at the Socratic Club made him even more determined to succeed in communicating Christian beliefs in an accessible and popular manner. Though he was convinced that philosophical work was entirely valid for a Christian, he gradually felt his calling was wider, especially now that philosophy in England had become increasingly analytical and narrow in focus. There was no diminishing of his view that humans are caught up in a battle going on between spiritual powers, some of which were intent on destroying humanity itself, and he itched to join the fray where the conflict was at its bloodiest and the need for reinforcements at its greatest. *The Screwtape Letters*, published in 1942, the year after the club started, had had an unexpected and dramatic success ("a reception I had never dreamed of," wrote Lewis). This response from the public, along with the earlier take up of *Out of the Silent Planet* before the war, was almost certainly a factor in his eventual resolve to concentrate on imaginative writing and popular theology as much as possible. This change of direction would not foreclose his academic literary writing, which was part of his job.

Exploring What Is Wrong with the World

The Cosmic Trilogy

I n his story *The Pilgrim's Regress*, C. S. Lewis pictured the attacks of hell on the human soul in a brilliant map of the world of thought in the 1920s and early 1930s, as we shall see at the beginning of part two. His concern over devilry and the spiritual battles that face everyone were shared by other writers of his time, and he would soon write more stories exposing the dark side. His friend J. R. R. Tolkien had the Dark Lord lurking in the gloomy haunts of Mirkwood in *The Hobbit*, published in 1937, who would become better known as Sauron in the later *The Lord of the Rings*. Charles Williams, befriended by Lewis in 1936, had been writing stories of devilry for a number of years. A mutual friend of Williams and Lewis, Dorothy L. Sayers, turned her attention to one of the definitive stories of selling one's soul to the devil, that of Dr. Faustus's pact with Satan. Though Sayers was never an Inkling (it was an informal all-male club, typical in respects of its time), because of her strong affinities and link with two of its key members, her absence would impoverish an exploration of modern and ancient devilry in the writings of Lewis and friends.

Sayers turned the Faust story into a play, performed shortly before World War II, because of its relevance, she felt, to the powers and forces leading the world toward destruction. She was a leading author in the golden age of murder mysteries—the interwar period—her characters Lord Peter Wimsey and Harriet Vane widely known. These detective stories implied a general acceptance of Jewish-Christian and similar values.[1] In writing the Faust play, Sayers had decided more or less to abandon her successful detective writing for drama and lay theology—theology written by those without theological training for a general readership. She wished to tackle the growing ignorance of what Lewis was later to call "Old Western values" in contemporary society. Lewis was not alone, therefore, in his increasing preoccupation with devilry and the dangers we face in trying to live a life marked by goodness rather than badness: facing powers that seem bent on destroying our very humanity and before which we can feel helpless.

Sayers's play was called *The Devil to Pay*, written for the 1939 Canterbury Festival—a festival that had already included plays by T. S. Eliot and Charles Williams, and which marked a resurgence in Christian drama. She reworked the legend of Faust, treated by Goethe and other significant writers, and included the standard characters Wagner, the demon Mephistopheles and Helen of Troy. Her challenge was "a question of supplying some kind of human interpretation of a supernatural legend."[2] In her preface Sayers points out,

> The legend of Faust remains one of the great stories of the world; a perpetual fascination to the poet, whose task is to deal with the eternities. For at the base of it lies the question of all questions: the nature of Evil and its place in the universe. Symbolise Evil, and call it the Devil, and then ask how the Devil came to be. Is he, as the Manichees taught, a power co-equal with and opposed to God? Or, if God is all-powerful, did He make the Devil, and if so, why, and with what justifi-

cation? Is the Devil a positive force, or merely a negation, the absence of Good? In what sense can a man be said to sell his soul to the Devil? What kind of man might do so, and, above all, for what inducement? Further, what meaning are we to place upon the concept of hell and damnation, with which the whole concept of the Devil is intimately bound up?

Questions such as these are answered by every generation in the light of its own spiritual needs and experience.[3]

Sayers's own take on the story is to depart from Goethe's warning against the fervent pursuit of knowledge for its own sake. "That is not our besetting sin," she wrote. Rather, she takes up the modern phenomenon of "the impulsive reformer, over-sensitive to suffering, impatient of the facts, eager to set the world right by sudden overthrow."[4] Such a reformer eventually falls into defeatism and escapes from reality. The form his escape takes is "very common in these times" (she writes in the late 1930s, of course, with tyrants at loose in Germany, Italy, Spain and Russia, and with catastrophic war impending). "It is," Sayers says, "the nostalgia of childhood, of the primitive, of the unconscious; the rejection of adult responsibility and the denial of all value to growth and time."[5] Evil cannot be undone, as if time could be reversed, she believed, but only purged and redeemed by Christ in history.

Sayers's friendship with Charles Williams, and particularly his book *The Figure of Beatrice*, led her to catch his infectious interest in Dante's *The Divine Comedy*. Dante's poem, in three parts, involves the poet's journey through hell and purgatory to paradise, and symbolizes the soul's journey to God, pulled by love. Like C. S. Lewis, in another story of a visit from hell to the outskirts of heaven, *The Great Divorce* (see chap. 8), Dante places himself in the story. *The Divine Comedy* ("comedy" meaning a happy ending) was an interest that was to become rife among the Inklings. In fact, Dante scholar Colin Hardie joined the group just after the war, and Tolkien became a member of the Oxford Dante Society in 1945, probably at Lewis's suggestion. Sayers's interest would lead to her embarking on a rhyme translation of *The Divine Comedy* in the war years, the first volume of which, *Hell*, being published in 1949. Dante writes of hell, purgatory and paradise in vivid imagery which has inspired writers and artists ever since. His triptych poem helped to shape the concern of the Inklings in wartime, and even before, with devilry, heaven, hell and purgatorial themes.

One morning, probably in the spring of 1936, Lewis and Tolkien were meeting together, as they were in a habit of doing, in Lewis's college rooms on a Monday morning. During their conversation, Lewis bewailed the fact that, these days, there was not enough of the stories they liked. Tolkien agreed. Lewis concluded that there was nothing for it but for them to write such stories themselves. The idea developed that one would write a story about journeying into space, and the other about time travel. They tossed for it, and Tolkien got the task of writing a time story, and Lewis a space adventure. The outcome was that their pledge resulted in Lewis writing a successful science fiction story, the first of three books in what eventually was dubbed, after Lewis's death, the "Cosmic Trilogy" (also sometimes called the "Ransom Trilogy" after its central character, Dr. Elwin Ransom, and sometimes the "Space Trilogy"). Tolkien, the perfectionist, followed more slowly. After a false start with "The Lost Road" (never finished), he eventually began writing *The Lord of the Rings*, which, coincidently, was eventually published in three volumes because of its length, and is haunted by the theme of time. Tolkien mentions in his letters on several occasions that *The Lord of the Rings* began with this pledge between the two friends.[6] Lewis seems to have begun his assignment immediately, it being published under two years later, with Tolkien not starting his until the end of the following year, and not publishing it until the mid 1950s (the first two volumes in 1954, and the final volume in 1955). Though concerned with space and time, respectively, both the Cosmic Trilogy and *The Lord of the Rings*, in their distinctive ways, explore devilry as a major theme. In this chapter we shall look at Lewis's venture into science fiction; we considered, of course, Tolkien's imagery of the dark side, which pervades *The Lord of the Rings*, in chapter four.

Exploration of devilry and the nature of evil, particularly their devastating impact on human life, is central to C. S. Lewis's science fiction. The first volume, *Out of the Silent Planet*, appeared just two years after Lewis had published a major study in medieval literature, *The Allegory of Love* (1936), a work of many years. This long task had led him to intense study of the worldview or world model of the period of the Middle Ages. Many years later this gave rise to his groundbreaking study *The Discarded Image* (published a year after his death). It is the splendid picture of the cosmos portrayed particularly in the later that which lies behind *Out of the Silent Planet* and the two subsequent science fiction stories. The themes of devilry, the desire of heaven and the lure of hell, damnation and salvation are introduced in this first story and extensively and more darkly developed in the following books.

Out of the Silent Planet

This first story sets the scene for the trilogy and is located on Mars (here called Malacandra). Lewis effortlessly and unobtrusively recreates the medieval picture of the cosmos in a modern science fiction tale. In Deep Heaven, each planet familiar to us is in fact guided by a spiritual intelligence, or Oyarsa, who, with the exception of the one concerned with Earth (the "Bent One"), are obedient to Maleldil the Young, their mysterious master. Earth is the "silent planet," Thulcandra, because it is cut off from the courtesy and order of Deep Heaven by a primeval disobedience. Lewis, with great effect, reverses the usual cosmic arrangement in the science fiction of his time, in which, predictably, evil and grave danger for humanity come from alien enemies in space. In *Out of the Silent Planet*, in stark contrast, evil resides on Earth, and our planet is therefore quarantined from the rest of the cosmos, the heavenly realm.

The angel-like beings whom Elwin Ransom first comes across on Malacandra are barely discernible to human eyes, though their voices are audible. The overall ruler of the "eldila" on a particular planet, the Oyarsa, has some similarity with classical gods associated with Mars, Venus, Mercury and other planets.

Lewis was astonished at the response of most reviewers. Half humorously, he complained in a letter in 1939, "You will be both grieved and amused to hear that out of about 60 reviews only two showed any knowledge that my idea of the fall of the Bent One was anything but an invention of my own."[7] He concluded that, these days, an unlimited amount of theology could be sneaked into people's minds using this kind of story without raising their barriers. This sort of response to *Out of the Silent Planet* was one of the things which made Lewis realize, after disappointing sales of his first fiction, *The Pilgrim's Regress*, that he might have something to offer in theological and ethical writing on a broad front.

The story introduces the main character in the trilogy, Dr. Elwin Ransom, a Tolkien-like philologist don from Cambridge University, who is kidnapped while on a walking holiday in the English Midlands and taken by spacecraft to the planet Malacandra by crooked entrepreneur Dick Devine and Professor Edward Weston, the latter a famous physicist and materialist. The duo are under a misapprehension that the unseen ruler of Malacandra wants a human sacrifice. The seeds of evil in Weston lie deeper than his willingness to sacrifice Ransom. This willingness is only a symptom of his perverse vision, which is to colonize the planets of space, mercilessly destroying native inhabitants for this greater "good" of populating the universe with human beings.

After escaping his captors, Ransom is at first terrified and disoriented by the red planet and its diversity of terrain and inhabitants—various forms of rational life related in a harmonious hierarchy. The inhabitants turn out to be civilized and amiable. Ransom, as a linguist, is soon able to pick up the rudiments of their language, Old Solar. Though Malacandra harbors an ancient and fading civilization, its harmony and racial pluralism provide a paradisiacal contrast to the woes of Ransom's native planet. In typical Lewis fashion, the reader is drawn into recognizing reality in a new and fresh way through the world of wonder he creates. Though not on Tolkien's scale, Malacandra is a subcreation or secondary world. Commenting on Lewis's skill in creating Malacandra (and, in his second volume, the planet Perelandra), Chad Walsh concludes, "Lewis's particular way of relating imaginary worlds to our empirical world—through theology and mythology as well as actual voyages back and forth—is distinctive and gives him a central claim to being master of this literary form."[8]

Ransom's change of perception, through whose eyes we see, leads us, as readers, to our own change of vision. In traveling to Malacandra, Ransom goes through a kind of new birth (there are a number of images of gestation and birth), which results in his new way of seeing the planet. Its wonder never leaves him. This is connected with overcoming his deep-rooted fears, such as of the apparent emptiness of space and of alien monsters.

In her study *Voyages to the Moon* (1948), Marjorie Hope Nicolson paid this tribute:

> *Out of the Silent Planet* is to me the most beautiful of all cosmic voyages and in some ways the most moving. . . . As C. S. Lewis, the Christian apologist, has added something to the long tradition, so C. S. Lewis, the scholar-poet, has achieved an effect in *Out of the Silent Planet* different from anything in the past. Earlier writers have created new worlds from legend, from

mythology, from fairy tale. Mr Lewis has created myth itself, myth woven of desire and aspirations deep-seated in some, at least, of the human race. . . . As I journey with him into worlds at once familiar and strange, I experience, as did Ransom, "a sensation not of following an adventure but of enacting a myth."[9]

Perelandra

Perelandra (*Voyage to Venus*) was not published until five years later, in 1943.[10] As its title suggests, the second volume of the trilogy is set on the planet Perelandra (Venus), an oceanic world of floating islands as well as fixed lands. It is a paradise world which evokes both the garden of the Hesperides of classical myth and the biblical vision of a new Earth.[11] The donnish hero of the first book, Dr. Elwin Ransom, has a more active role in his second adventure. Prepared by his experiences on Malacandra, Ransom is transported to Perelandra to counter the attacks of the forces of evil now possessing the human form of his old enemy, Weston. Instead of traveling there in a womb-like space ship, Ransom is carried in a casket by supernatural means. In the first book, he was, in a sense, reborn. In the second, he must accept the necessity of death, symbolized in the coffin. Perelandra, Ransom discovers, has its own green-fleshed and human equivalent of Adam and Eve.[12] The setting is poetic and beautifully created. Perelandra has unspoiled ecology, which includes the communion between the Green Lady and her husband, and the animal and fish life of the planet. Their planetary home is intended to contrast with the havoc of sin on our world. Perelandra presents a forceful and inspiring image of perfection, where natural and spiritual are one. But its watery Eden is threatened by evil even more insidious than that which ruined the first humans on our planet. Instead of a serpent able to voice the devil's words, on Perelandra a human being (albeit increasingly possessed by the devil) speaks the subtle temptations of the Evil One to the Green Lady. In *The Screwtape Letters* we are let into the ploys of devilry via Screwtape's letters. In *Perelandra* we overhear the plausible conversations of malice embodied in no less than Professor Weston's possessed frame as he speaks with the innocent first woman of the oceanic planet.

World War II raged while Ransom was taken to Perelandra. He was away for a whole year. On his return he recounted to his friends what happened. The account forms the basis of Lewis's book as if he had heard the narration, for the friends, we are told, are C. S. Lewis himself and Dr. "Humphrey" Havard, another of the Inklings.

Ransom told his friends that after dropping through the Venusian atmosphere, he had found himself in a

> delicious coolness. . . . He was riding the foamless swell of an ocean, fresh and cool after the fierce temperatures of Heaven, but warm by earthly standards—as warm as a shallow bay with sandy bottom in a sub-tropical climate. As he rushed smoothly up the great convex hillside of the next wave he got a mouthful of the water. It was hardly at all flavoured with salt; it was drinkable—like fresh water and only, by an infinitesimal degree, less insipid. Though he had not been aware of thirst till now, his drink gave him a quite astonishing pleasure. It was almost like meeting Pleasure itself for the first time.[13]

Paradise is brilliantly evoked by Lewis's descriptions.

One fascinating feature of Perelandra is its floating islands, which follow the contours of the sea, with hills becoming valleys and valleys hills in a continual shift of shape. The exception is when the ocean is still and the island becomes flat. Much that happens to Ransom takes place on the islands. In contrast is the fixed land, upon which the newly created green humans of the planet are as yet forbidden to dwell, although they can visit but not remain there overnight. This command forms the basis of a reenactment of the temptation of Eve. There are differences, however, most importantly as a result of the sacrifice of Maleldil the Young long ago on Thulcandra (the "silent planet," Earth). The sedentary scholar Ransom has to play an active role, much to his alarm, in frustrating the devilish plans of the bent Oyarsa of Earth to corrupt the unspoiled world. It is on one of the floating islands, reminiscent of the garden of the Hesperides of classical myth, that Ransom encounters the beautiful Green Lady. Her constant animal companions include a small dragon with scales of red gold. She was "green like the beautifully coloured green beetle in an English garden." She was like "a goddess carved apparently out of green stone, yet alive." As Ransom often found happening, what was myth in our world could be fact in others. When she started laughing uncontrollably at his strange appearance (one half of his body had been scorched by the sun in space while traveling in the casket) he realized that she was fully human. Humorously, she went on to nickname him "Piebald," after a Perelandrian flower. Several times the narrator refers to her as human.

Professor Weston, in contrast to Ransom, arrived in a conventional spacecraft of his own making. He lost no time in engaging the Green Lady in complex and subtle arguments, designed to wear down her resistance to the temptation to disobey the command not to live on the fixed lands. Ransom intervenes as best he can with counterargument, as the innocent Green Lady can only be swayed by rational debate, albeit often couched in poetic language. Unlike the possessed scientist, Ransom suffers the disadvantage of sleeping from sheer exhaustion. He has to act as a human agent on behalf of all that is good and uncorrupted, rather than merely as a tool of the guiding Oyarsa or guardian spirit of Perelandra. Those are the rules of this spiritual battle.

Lewis's story carries his belief, much discussed in the medieval period that he loved, about what evil really is. For him, like the great Christian thinkers who influenced that period, evil is the negation of what is, rather than existing in its own right. Evil is an abnormality, lacking substance and weight, drawing its terrible power from the goodness that it is perverting. On the planet of Perelandra, the only word of Old Solar that readily describes evil is therefore "bentness." Hebrew, the language of the Genesis narrative that describes the fall of Adam and Eve, expresses evil with a metaphor rather like the Perelandrian "bentness." According to a Bible dictionary, the Hebrew "word [ra'] comes from a root meaning 'to spoil,' 'to break in pieces': being broken and so made worthless. It is essentially what is unpleasant, disagreeable, offensive. The word binds together the evil deed and its consequences."[14]

In *Perelandra* Lewis tries to capture the true freedom that the unfallen Green Lady enjoys in her full humanity. Ransom is trying to warn her of something outside her experience—evil—that has come to the planet in order to destroy her perfect state. He helps her to realize that her self is distinct from that of the Creator of the worlds, Maleldil. It is an awareness of otherness. She needs this awareness in order to protect herself against Professor Weston's devilry.

> "I thought," she said [to Ransom], "that I was carried in the will of Him I love, but now I see that I walk with it. . . . How has He made me so separate from Himself? How did it enter His mind to conceive such a thing? The world is so much larger than I thought. I thought we went along paths—but it seems there are no paths. The going itself is the path."[15]

Ransom is acutely aware that it is possible for a being who is perfectly good, and in a perfect environment, to create evil. In her conversation with Ransom, the Green Lady of Perelandra suddenly understands how it is possible for evil to come out of goodness:

> "What you have made me see," answered the Lady, "is as plain as the sky, but I never saw it before. Yet it has happened every day. One goes into the forest to pick food and already the

thought of one fruit rather than another has grown up in one's mind. . . . And if you wished—if it were possible to wish—you could keep it there. You could send your soul after the good you had expected, instead of turning it to the good you had got. You could refuse the real good; you could make the real fruit taste insipid by thinking of the other."[16]

As always, Lewis places everlasting consequences upon small, ordinary choices.

In the situation of Eden known to Ransom on Earth, the first man and woman faced the test of being forbidden only the fruit of one tree, the tree of the knowledge of good and evil. The test includes a warning and the opportunity to freely obey out of love. Love would have no meaning if humans were programmed as robots or were puppets.

Lewis parallels this test very astutely in *Perelandra*. What is myth can be fact—on Earth at the beginning of history is a tree, on Perelandra in the opening years of its history is a different prohibition but the same principle. On its oceanic planet the command has been given not to live on the mainland, the Fixed Island. Remember, the satanic tempter here is embodied in the dehumanized Weston rather than being in the form of a serpent through whom the devil gives voice.

"Lady," said Ransom, "if I speak, will you hear me?" "Gladly, Piebald."

"This man [Weston] has said that the law against living on the Fixed Island is different from the other Laws, because it is not the same for all worlds and because we cannot see the goodness in it. And so far he says well. But then he says that it is thus different in order that you may disobey it. But there might be another reason."

"Say it, Piebald."

"I think He made one law of that kind in order that there might be obedience. In all these other matters what you call obeying Him is but doing what seems good in your own eyes also. Is love content with that?"

The Green Lady is delighted by Ransom's argument and remarks, "We cannot walk out of Maleldil's will: but He has given us a way to walk out of our will. And there could be no such way except a command like this."[17]

Eventually Ransom realizes, to his dismay, that he must engage Weston in a physical fight to the death. Weston, given over to the devil, is now an "Un-man." In the bitter struggle, Ransom receives a wound to his heel that will never mend. The principle here of course is that it is sometimes necessary to fight evil and the bad by force. On a social rather than individual level, it may involve defensive war or imprisoning wrongdoers. The Perelandian arguments relate therefore to Lewis's views on warfare; why he found it impossible to be a pacifist, though he strongly felt that there were moral limits to the practice of warfare, even where it was a necessary evil.[18] Ransom had to add physical resistance to argument against the destructive half-truths and malicious deceptions of the Un-man who had once been Weston. He had to fight Weston hand to hand. Lewis continued his exploration of evil in the final part of his science fiction trilogy, *That Hideous Strength* (1945), set several years later, just after the war.

That Hideous Strength

In this "modern fairy tale for grown-ups," Dr. Elwin Ransom is involved in adventures on Earth, known to the rest of the planets as the "silent planet," cut off from the heaven that surrounds it in the solar system and the wider universe. He has a directorial role as the head of a small community a little like a religious order, but which has a variety of members, including a highly intelligent skeptic. Ransom in fact has been revealed as the Pendragon of Logres (the spiritual or real England), the latest in a succession from the time of King Arthur. The setting is a small East Midland university town of Edgestow. This fictional town has a small federation of colleges like (on a larger scale) Oxford and Cambridge and (on a smaller scale) Durham University. The "progressive element" among the fellows of Bracton College engineer the sale of an ancient piece of property called Bragdon Wood to the N.I.C.E., the National Institute of Co-ordinated Experiments. This element represents all that Lewis disliked in university politics.

According to Arthurian legend, the magician Merlin lay secretly in a trance within the Wood, his "sleeping" body preserved from aging. In the story he awakes and plays his pivotal role in the battle against the "hideous strength" of the N.I.C.E., or rather the demonic powers behind the N.I.C.E.

The N.I.C.E. is a sinister, totalitarian organization of technocrats: scientists given over to the pragmatic use of technology for social and individual control, free from moral constraints as understood by ordinary people. Deeply involved in the Institute is Dick Devine, now Lord Feverstone, first encountered by Ransom before the war as his kidnapper, along with Professor Weston, stealing him off to the planet Malacandra. Members of the N.I.C.E. are seeking nothing less than to reboot the human race. They wish to purge it of its universal values of freedom and dignity. One N.I.C.E. member, Filostrato, reveals what he considers to be its inner purpose to Mark Studdock, a Fellow in Sociology at Bracton College:

> This Institute . . . is for something better than housing and vaccinations and faster trains and curing people of cancer. It is for the conquest of death. . . . It is to bring out of that cocoon of organic life which sheltered the babyhood of mind the New

Man, the man who will not die, the artificial man, free from Nature. Nature is the ladder we have climbed up by, now we kick her away.

The appliance of science in technology is allowed to have a totalitarian rule; true science is distorted into technocracy. In the process, new demons take possession. They are in fact the old demons using a new strategy. This time the domination of the whole human race appears to be within their grasp.

Mark Studdock is duped into working for the N.I.C.E., whereas his wife, Jane, a research student in English literature, finds herself helping the other side, led by Ransom. Her gift of second sight helps to locate Merlin and to provide vital intelligence. Merlin's ancient magic, linked into the power of the eldila of Deep Heaven, overcomes the evil of the N.I.C.E. In a satirical climax, Merlin revives the curse of Babel, confused speech, as a fitting judgment on people who have despised ordinary humanity.

This book, as a sequel to the previous stories, set on other planets, brings matters "down to earth," under the influence of Lewis's Inklings friend Charles Williams on the story. (In fact, while Ransom the philologist is Tolkien-like in the first two stories, he is more like Charles Williams in this one.) We learn more of the significance of its setting, Thulcandra, the silent planet Earth, so called because it is cut off by evil from the beatific language as well as the worlds of Deep Heaven. In another sense, matters are brought "down to earth" because Lewis takes pains in characterizing the marriage and personalities of Mark and Jane Studdock. In the style of Charles Williams, the supernatural world impinges on the everyday world of ordinary people. Lewis shows the same deft touch in portraying basic details of human life that he displays in *The Screwtape Letters*. In both, ordinary living is the theater of damnation and salvation. There are other Williams-like touches also. Jane, like Damaris in Charles Williams's novel *The Place of the Lion*, is engaged in literary research without realizing the metaphysical realities that lie behind old authors like John Donne or Peter Abelard. Also C. S. Lewis makes use of the mythical geography of Logres, the Arthurian matter that is the focus of Williams's unfinished cycle of poems.

As Lewis makes clear in his preface, his story illustrates the point that he made in one of his most forceful studies of ethics, *The Abolition of Man* (see appendix 2). This is that a world which rejects objective principles of right and wrong, beauty and ugliness, also rejects what constitutes humankind's very nature and creates an unhumanity. The new society projected by the N.I.C.E. is the corruption writ large of the Un-man of Perelandra, who was once a brilliant scientist.

As a study of evil *That Hideous Strength* shows how wickedness sows the seeds of its own destruction. Professor Weston's forays into space with evil intent had allowed the ending of an ancient prohibition. This was that no inhabitants of Deep Heaven would ever come to the quarantined planet Earth until the very end of things. Now that bent humans had tried to contaminate unfallen worlds such as Mars and Venus, however, the eldila of Deep Heaven could release their good powers through a suitable human agent—Merlin.

The novel has been criticized for being overcomplex in structure. It has, for example, an uneasy mixture of satire and serious study of damnation, a mixture that worked well in *The Screwtape Letters*. Nevertheless, it is one of Lewis's fictions that can make the most impact on some readers, revealing a power to portray ordinary human beings in a "realistic" setting. It is plausible as an anti-utopian parable of our times, like Aldous Huxley's *Brave New World* (1932) and George Orwell's *Nineteen Eighty-Four* (1949), and takes the genre forward.

Orwell wrote a favorable newspaper review of the book shortly after the atomic bombings of Hiroshima and Nagasaki. Though he disliked the supernatural elements in Lewis's story and thought the story would be better without them, he recommended it as a book "worth reading" to the readers of the *Manchester Evening News*.[19] He gave a good sketch of the book and its plausibility in the light of the events in Japan a few days before:

> [Lewis's] book describes the struggle of a little group of sane people against a nightmare that nearly conquers the world. A company of mad scientists—or, perhaps, they are not mad, but have merely destroyed in themselves all human feeling, all notion of good and evil—are plotting to conquer Britain, then the whole planet, and then other planets, until they have brought the universe under their control. . . . Man, in short, is to storm the heavens and overthrow the gods, or even to become a god himself. . . . Plenty of people in our age do entertain the monstrous dreams of power that Mr. Lewis attributes to his characters, and we are within sight of the time when such dreams will be realisable.

Like Tolkien and Lewis, and other contemporary writers like William Golding, T. H. White and Kurt Vonnegut, George Orwell had a clear sense of the challenge of grappling with modern evil in literature.[20]

part
two

The Intersection of
Good and Evil

Progress and Regress in the Journey of Life

The Pilgrim's Regress

In the first chapter of part one, our exploration of C. S. Lewis's experiences in two periods of world war revealed the great change in his understanding of evil and the struggle to be good. Soon after his conversion to Christianity, Lewis turned to fiction and an attempt to map the twists and turns of his road to faith in the 1920s and early 1930s. The result was called *The Pilgrim's Regress*. The very approach he took, that of a journey on foot along mainly rural highways and byways, belonged to that period as well. Walking holidays were popular with the middle classes and intelligentsia, as part of a new nostalgia for nature, and accounts of journeys and the countryside were popular. Journalist H. V. Morton's *In Search of England* (1927) was a bestseller.

Valentine Cunningham points out the impact of this phenomenon on the literature of the 1930s:

> Walking and mapping and traversing landscapes couldn't be more fundamental to '30s literature's sense of itself, to the '30s writers' typical envisaging of their art and their politics as

being on the road, on the way, into or across new country. . . .
These literary mapmakers seem now, of course, a lot like their
immediate predecessors, the Georgian ramblers and walkers,
the Hilaire Bellocs and the Richard Jefferies, who obviously
engendered the brisk progressions from country pub to
country pub that characterized the holidays of C. S. Lewis and
his friends, and that came increasingly to attract C. Day Lewis.[1]

C. S. Lewis and his friends went on many walking vacations. It is
perhaps no coincidence that much of Tolkien's *The Hobbit*, which
was being composed in the early 1930s, is made up of a long journey,
much of it on foot, by Bilbo Baggins and a party of dwarves through
the Shire, up and then under the Misty Mountains and across
Mirkwood and beyond. Each stage of the journey is beautifully de-
scriptive. Lewis had read Tolkien's manuscript by the time he wrote
The Pilgrim's Regress.

Although Lewis's story shows the marks of being his first prose
fiction, it has a great deal of charm, and many like to reread it. Although it describes the period after World War I, much of what it
portrays illuminates ideas of our own time. To bring out its importance in exploring the dangers of slipping hellward or the difficulties of traveling heavenward, some description of the basic story,
and the kind of story it is, is necessary. A noticeable feature of the
story is that the lure to John, the traveler, of byroads from the main
road has a demonic dimension—that is, a subtle and sinister
twisting of natural curiosity. The byroads are part of hell's devices
to capture the human soul, just as those off the narrow path are in
John Bunyan's *The Pilgrim's Progress.*

Lewis's allegory tells the story of John, who is born in Puritania, a
country of strict moral rules. John is taught early to fear the Landlord
of the region. One of his childhood horrors was a fear that, for things
he couldn't avoid doing, the Landlord would take him and shut him

up "forever and ever in a black hole full of snakes and scorpions as large as lobsters—for ever and ever."[2] Then, one day, John glimpses an island in a vision. From the first moment that he sees it, he is gripped with an intense longing to find it. When he is old enough he sets out on foot to find it. There are many distractions to lure him off from the westward-bound main road, either to the north or the south.

On his journey, he encounters characters such as Mr. Enlightenment from the city of Claptrap, Mr. Vertue, who becomes John's companion, and Media Halfways, from the city of Thrill. Later, John is imprisoned by the Spirit of the Age, and rescued by Reason, a tall, armored woman in a cloak of blue. She teaches him some important principles and directs him back to the Main Road:

> Then the rider threw back the cloak and a flash of steel smote light into John's eyes and on the giant's face. John saw that it was a woman in the flower of her age: she was so tall that she seemed to him a Titaness, a sun-bright virgin clad in complete steel, with a sword naked in her hand.[3]

John's capture by the Spirit of the Age is a good representative of many vivid vignettes in the story. He was walking tiredly in the darkness on a road to the north of the main road, a road which led into a long, rocky valley. There were high cliffs to either side of him. At the far end of the valley the only way on was through a pass, visible in the moonlight. Also visible was the shadow of a man's head cast by a mountain John had passed. When he came across some armed men, they arrested him on the orders of the giant called the Spirit of the Age. The apparent mountain was in fact the unmoving giant. John was chained by a young man called Sigismund Enlightenment and led to a prison in a hillside facing the ever watchful giant.

Sigismund's name, and the fact that he loyally serves the giant, the Spirit of the Age, shows clearly that he represents the new psychology of Freud. John's captor in fact represents the modern psychology, which in the time Lewis was writing reduced human desires and aspirations to mere wish fulfillment. Indeed, as Sigismund dragged John to jail he set to attacking his motives for making his journey, particularly undermining his longing for the island he had glimpsed.

In the prison were many captives, men and women of all ages. It happened that whenever the Spirit of the Age opened his eyes and looked at the unfortunate prisoners, their innards were made visible, so that they looked to John like demons. He could see their lungs like sponges and intestines like snakes. Through their faces their skulls were visible, and through the skulls their brains could be seen. One man's large tumor was revealed. When he looked down, John could see his own insides.

John's torment went on for many days, until he cried out, "It is the black hole. There may be no Landlord, but it is true about the black hole. I am mad. I am dead. I am in hell for ever."[4]

The jailer, when he brought food for the prisoners, made a habit of poisoning their view of what they were eating with his comments. If the meal was meat, he reminded them they were eating corpses or would describe methods of slaughter. If eggs, he would point out what eggs really were and make jokes at the expense of the female prisoners. One day, however, when he represented milk as one of a number of indelicate secretions of a cow, John's reason awoke, and he challenged Sigismund about confusing what in nature is refuse and what is stored up as food. Dung and milk were not the same thing. The argument continued until the jailer finally dragged John to the feet of the giant for punishment. It was at that stage that the blue clad figure of Reason slayed the giant and rescued John.

After much traveling and many more adventures, John finds the road abruptly cut off by a vast canyon. He at first refuses the help of Mother Kirk (representing "Christianity as against unbelief")[5] and has many adventures as he looks for a way down first to the north and then to the south of the main road. After becoming lost and calling for help, John is aided first by the hermit History and then Reason once more. He finds Mr. Vertue in the presence of Mother Kirk, and both follow her guidance and reach the other side of the canyon. From here John can see the sea and his island. The two are given a guide to lead them back across the world, for the island in fact is the other side of the mountains near Puritania, not an island at all. Going back is the necessary "regress" of the title. John's idea of the Landlord has turned out to be false, and the home of the Landlord in those mountains is to be John's as well. In fact, in all of John's journey back, he sees the world in a very different way, shorn of the illusions of the various modern movements, trends or fashions.

C. S. Lewis came to Christian faith in 1931, when he was thirty-two. He had before then come to the conclusion that the modern world was out of continuity with the Western past. Lewis placed his times (the 1920s and early 1930s) firmly in the context of the larger cosmic battle between good and evil mentioned in chapter one. *The Pilgrim's Regress* pictures this conflict in a symbolic geography, his own *mappa mundi* (world map), which has some affinities with Tolkien's depiction of Middle-earth. He was familiar with at least the First Age of Middle-earth through reading and having read to him material from *The Silmarillion* as it was taking shape and being refined. In both writers the inspiration for such a middle world came from the thought, art and writing of the Middle Ages, the area of their scholarly interest. The spiritual context of the conflicts that raged in their fictions was heightened for both by their experiences of battle in World War I.

A rather similar symbolic geography to that in *The Pilgrim's Regress* is found in his later Narnian Chronicles, which will be featured more in chapter nine. In the worlds depicted by Lewis in his first fiction and the much later Chronicles of Narnia, the attacks from evil powers come from the north and south. In the specifically allegorical *The Pilgrim's Regress*, this represents a twofold onslaught on what Lewis calls the "two sides of our nature," the mind and the physical sensations.

As set out in *The Pilgrim's Regress*, both the "north" and the "south" tendencies actually dehumanize us, a thesis he was to explore in the philosophical book *The Abolition of Man* ten years later (see appendix 2). To remain human we have no choice but the straight and narrow, the "Main Road": "With both the 'North' and 'South,'" Lewis writes, "a man has, I take it, only one concern—to avoid them and hold the Main Road. . . . We were made to be neither cerebral men nor visceral men, but Men. Not beasts nor angels but Men—things at once rational, and animal."[6] In his philosophical treatise he refers to an ancient index of the human body, with "the chest" as the healthy and wholesome balance of life. The chest, the ancients argued, is the seat of balance in the mature human being. It harmonizes our cerebral and emotional aspects, our heads and hearts. For Lewis, modern people increasingly lack "chests"—a process he warned would eventually lead to the abolition of humanity.

Lewis further explains the map as a scheme of "the Holy War as I see it." Significantly, there are military railways both to the north and south. These were meant, he says, "to symbolize the double attack from hell on the two sides of our nature [the mind and the physical sensations]. It was hoped that the roads spreading out from each of the enemy railheads would look like claws or tentacles reaching out into the country of Man's Soul." Theologian J. I. Packer points out that the idea of the Holy War, drawn from John Bunyan and others, as well as Lewis's war experience, not only informs *The Pilgrim's Regress* but "gives shape and perspective to Lewis's output as a whole."[7] The attack on the soul from north and south represent, in Lewis's words, "equal and opposite evils, each continually strengthened and made plausible by its critique of the other." The northern people are cold, with "rigid systems whether sceptical or dogmatic, Aristocrats, Stoics, Pharisees, Rigorists, signed and sealed members of highly organized 'Parties.'" The emotional southerners are the opposite, "boneless souls whose doors stand open day and night to almost every visitant, but always with the readiest welcome for those . . . who offer some sort of intoxication. . . . Every feeling is justified by the mere fact that it is felt: for a Northerner, every feeling on the same ground is suspect."[8]

Like the correspondence between devils in his later book *The Screwtape Letters*, *The Pilgrim's Regress* focused in on the individual human soul, whereas the later Narnian Chronicles would be somewhat more concerned with the nature of human and Christian society and the meaning of history, though nevertheless featuring the temptations and trials of individuals (such as Eustace, the young King Caspian and Jill Pole). The green and pleasant land of Narnia would represent a virtuous civilization threatened by enemies from the cold north and hot south. From the north would come a Snow Queen and giants, and to the south the warmongering Calormenes ("Calor" meaning "hot" in Latin).

At a deeper level, John's quest for the island is a fine embodiment of the theme of joy, which is so central in Lewis's autobiography, *Surprised by Joy*, and which is a signature theme in many of his books. The quest helps John to avoid the various snares and dangers he encounters. In portraying his own quest for joy on the dangerous road between heaven and hell, Lewis pours himself into *The Pilgrim's Regress*, something he rarely did to this extent in his writings. When the book had only minimal sales, he was deeply disappointed, though he soon reasoned why its take up by the public had been so small.

While writing his first prose fiction, Lewis failed to realize what demands he was making on his readers. His storytelling skills developed gradually, as part of a determination to communicate to ordinary mortals rather than donnish friends. Much of the honing he accomplished he owed to his friends, the Inklings, who formed from existing friends and new ones within a couple of years or so after his conversion to Christianity. His increasing ability to communicate in his writing that was aimed outside of a scholarly audience, both fiction and nonfiction, also owed a great deal to his letter writing, including the large proportion of letters written to his Ulster friend Arthur Greeves, who was not an academic.

Twenty years after writing *The Pilgrim's Regress*, Lewis was able to frankly admit in a letter to a reader, "I don't wonder that you got fogged in *The Pilgrim's Regress*. It was my first religious book and I didn't then know how to make things easy. I was not even trying to very much, because in those days I never dreamed I would become a 'popular' author."[9] In the new, third edition of *The Pilgrim's Regress*, Lewis decided to provide a detailed preface and notes to the chapters to help his readers with the more obscure points of the allegory. It is in fact best to enjoy the book as a story and not be too concerned with the meaning of every allusion.

His intuitive sense of the drama involved in even the most ordinary people in the journey between heaven and hell would be realized fully and spectacularly in his *The Screwtape Letters*, published less than ten years later, which we explored in chapter two, and also in his dream fantasy *The Great Divorce*—as we shall see in chapter eight.

The Divide Between Good and Bad

Tolkien's "Leaf by Niggle" and Lewis's *The Great Divorce*

Like C. S. Lewis, J. R. R. Tolkien believed that there was a great divide between good and evil. This divide, they believed, faces all of humanity, however humble and ordinary our lives. It is evident in our struggles to live a good life, and the achievement of heaven is impossible, the two friends believed, without divine grace.[1] Both Lewis and Tolkien were deeply familiar with the great medieval poem *The Divine Comedy*, in which its author, Dante, imagines himself on a journey that takes him through hell and then purgatory to heaven. Tolkien wrote the story of a painter called Niggle and his journey from this world to heaven. The story, which was published in the *Dublin Review* in 1945, is called "Leaf by Niggle," for reasons we shall see. It was necessary for Niggle to spend a period in purgatory to be prepared for heaven. Tolkien felt the need for purgatory because of the gap between our present state and the exalted state of living in the heavenly country. There are a number of autobiographical elements in the story, which is very unusual for Tolkien, as well as elements of allegory, which he usually disliked.

"Leaf by Niggle"

In the story, Niggle, a little man and an artist, knew that he would one day have to make a journey. Many matters got in the way of his painting, such as the demands of his neighbor, Mr. Parish, who had a lame leg. Niggle was soft-hearted and rather lazy.

Niggle was concerned to finish one painting in particular. This had started as an illustration of a leaf caught in the wind, and then became a tree. Through gaps in the leaves and branches a forest and a whole world opened up. As the painting grew (with other, smaller paintings tacked on) Niggle had had to move it into a specially built shed on his potato plot.

Eventually Niggle fell ill after getting soaked in a storm while running an errand for Mr. Parish. Then the dreaded Inspector visited to tell him that the time had come for him to set out on the journey.

Taking a train, his first stop (which seemed to last for a century) was at the Workhouse, as Niggle had not brought any belongings. He worked very hard there on various chores. At last, one day, when he had been ordered to rest, he overheard two voices discussing his case. One of them spoke up for him. It was time for gentler treatment, he said.

Niggle was allowed to resume his journey in a small train that led him to the familiar world depicted in his painting of long ago, and to his tree, now complete. "It's a gift!" he exclaimed. Niggle then walked toward the forest (which had tall mountains behind). He realized that there was unfinished work here, and that Parish could help him—his old neighbor knew a lot about plants, earth and trees. At this realization he came across Parish, and the two of them worked busily together. At last, Niggle felt that it was time to move on into the mountains. Parish wished to remain behind to await his wife. It turned out that the region they had worked in together was called Niggle's Country, much to their surprise. A guide led Niggle into the mountains.

Long before, back in the town near where Niggle and Parish had lived before the journey, a fragment of Niggle's painting had survived and been hung in the town museum, titled simply, "Leaf by Niggle." It depicted a spray of leaves with a glimpse of a mountain peak.

Niggle's Country became a popular place to send travelers as a holiday, for refreshment and convalescence, and as a splendid introduction to the mountains.

Tolkien's little story suggests the link between art and reality. Even in heaven there will be place for the artist to add his or her own touch to the created world. In the allegory, the distant mountains represent heaven. The workhouse represents Tolkien's orthodox Roman Catholic view of a purgatorial state between this life and entry into heaven. Many other allegorical elements could be interpreted, such as the journey indicates death. The story beautifully provides heaven as the ultimate context of human life and endeavor, and offers hope in the struggles of ordinary life.

The Great Divorce: A Dream

Closely related to "Leaf by Niggle" is C. S. Lewis's fiction *The Great Divorce*, serialized during the war and published exactly a year after "Leaf by Niggle," in January 1946. It much more clearly highlights the great divide between hell and heaven, and goodness and badness. Whereas Tolkien's story focused mainly on Niggle and his neighbor Parish, Lewis's spotlight is on a number of people from various walks of life. The title, Lewis points out, is a response to the poet William Blake's *The Marriage of Heaven and Hell*. Whatever the great poet meant by this, Lewis thought it a dangerous error to think that the two could be reconciled, and any attempt to doesn't face up to the absolute either-or that is a feature of the reality. As usual with such of his books, he made it clear that he was not trying to put over factual information about the actual state of the afterlife, but presenting a fiction or, as he preferred to put it, a supposal, supposing this or that as the basis for the story. In this case, suppose inhabitants of hell are allowed an excursion to the borderlands of heaven. In fact, Lewis frames the story as a dream, from which he abruptly awakens at the end to the familiar wartime sound of a siren's howl. This is reminiscent of the close of *The Screwtape Letters*, in which the earthly protagonist dies in an air raid.

As in *The Screwtape Letters*, the spotlight is on the danger of damnation of a person (one person in the *Letters* and a number of people in *The Great Divorce*). *The Great Divorce* however takes the very opposite perspective to *The Screwtape Letters*. It is concerned with attempts to save people from damnation, rather than to guarantee torment. In *The Great Divorce* we see things at least partly from the viewpoint of the "Bright Ones," the inhabitants of the heavenly country, who try to persuade the visitors to stay. Though there is the difference that the subject of demonic attention in the *Letters* is still alive and the visitors from hell in *The Great Divorce* are in an afterlife, the tourists continue acting in the patterns and habits of their previous, earthly lives. In the dream story, they are still as yet free to choose heaven and not return to hell.

Tolkien refers to Lewis's story being read in installments to the Inklings during 1944, in letters to his son, Christopher, serving in South Africa with the RAF. He describes it as "C. S. L.'s new moral allegory or 'vision,' based on the medieval fancy of the *Refrigerium*, by which lost souls have an occasional holiday in Paradise." Originally the story was titled *Who Goes Home?* Thinking of a fellow Inkling, Hugo Dyson, Tolkien suggested in one meeting that it rather should be called *Hugo's Home*.

As well as being read in episodes to the Inklings, *The Great Divorce* was read occasionally to Tolkien alone. It explores the destination of the human self in heaven or hell, but with the twist that the twilight zone of hell also resembles purgatory for the soul that escapes it. Lewis modestly places himself in the twilight zone in which the story opens, as narrator telling his dream. *The Great Divorce* has some affinities with *The Screwtape Letters*, but its perspective is very different. It is not the complete contrast that Lewis would have liked to be able to render—that of the angelic perspective on human struggles in place of the diabolical. However, the solid beings who come to the fringes of heaven to meet the shadowy souls visiting from hell give much of this opposite perspective in a humanized way. As we saw, the devilish take on the tempting of what Screwtape called the "human vermin" was also personified, with Wormwood the junior tempter being the nephew of the senior devil, and with the administration of hell appearing rather like a mixture of bureaucratic regime and winner-takes-all modern company.

Like *The Screwtape Letters*, *The Great Divorce* also concerns the ways of heaven and hell, and the radical differences between them. Lewis intentionally casts his story in the form of a dream because he does not wish his reader to think that information is being presented about the actual state after death. This of course does not mean that Lewis denies an actual heaven and hell. The opposite is true. He is in fact concerned in this story to show their plausibility and reality, focused on a credible account of the effects of self-centeredness in human living and relationships, even the most loving of them.

The story opens in a gray town, with Lewis standing in a bus queue on a pavement in a long, shabby street. He had wandered for hours in similar, mean streets. Hell is an endless conurbation of perpetual twilight, where people move further and further away from each other. To be made, a new building just has to be thought, but lacks sufficient substance to keep out the rain that constantly falls.

Anyone in hell who wishes can take a bus trip to heaven, or at least to its outlands. Lewis takes such a trip with a varied collection of ghosts. Upon arrival in the hinterlands of heaven the passengers find it painfully solid, hard and bright in comparison to hell. Solid People who have traveled vast distances to meet the ghosts try to persuade them to stay, pointing out that they will gradually adjust to heaven and become more solid as they forsake particular follies that hold them back from heaven. In each case, making such a choice means a self-surrender. The inner conflicts this creates in the spectral visitors are acutely recognizable from ordinary human experience in this present life. Much of the story is taken up with encounters between solid people and ghosts, who were friends, relations or spouses on earth.

Out of many that take place, these vignettes are the particular encounters that are overheard by the narrator, Lewis. One such is a conversation between Dick, a member of the solid, heavenly inhabitants, and the wraith of a bishop. Dick had been a clergyman on earth. Ironically the bishop chides him for entertaining a "narrow-minded" belief in a literal heaven and hell toward the end of his life. When Dick replies, "Wasn't I right?" the bishop is shocked.

Another wraith on a trip from the gray town to the outskirts of heaven is called simply "the Dwarf," suggesting in this context the crumbling of his humanity. Back on earth he had been Frank, husband of Sarah Smith from Golder's Green, in London. The Dwarf is accompanied by a tall ghost, the "Tragedian," who represents the theatrical, posing side of Frank. Sarah Smith fails to persuade the Dwarf to enter heaven, and all that remains in the end is the tall, unreal, posing actor. What Frank has lost becomes clear when Sarah's full reality is displayed: there is a magnificent procession in her honor.

Lewis himself meets the nineteenth-century Scottish writer he considered his master, George MacDonald, who explains many mysteries of salvation and damnation to him. The encounter between Sarah Smith and Frank, which fails to persuade Frank to stay, leads Lewis to ask some searching questions of MacDonald. Lewis particularly questions him about his apparent universalism, the belief that all people will be saved. Here, and throughout the story, it is clear that hell and the choice to keep living a self-centered life are only possible through the misuse of free will.

The difficulties of salvation when the self is fixed on itself are clear in the story. Out of all the bus passengers, only one accepts the invitation to stay in heaven, after allowing a red lizard of lust perched on his shoulder to be destroyed by a colossal angel. Lewis's portrait of the apostate bishop, for instance, strikes home sharply. He returns to hell to read a paper to its theological society! Lewis's story vividly illustrates that the road to life is narrow, and the way is broad that leads to the destruction of all that is human.

As in *The Screwtape Letters*, Lewis in *The Great Divorce* highlights practical matters of life like family problems, selfishness, disagreement, greed and the persistence of bad habits. He does this with the sure touch that we saw in *The Screwtape Letters*. The orientation of the self is at the center of what goes wrong in human life. For Lewis, universalism is ruled out by the reality of human will; hell is in fact chosen by the damned. The door is shut from the inside.

In Lewis's dream story, people of the heavenly country known to the day-trippers try to persuade them to stay. Attempting to stay is clearly a purgatorial process that is painful and discomforting, but one which the solid people testify is achievable. In Lewis's view, the inhabitants of hell who remain there are successful rebels. MacDonald in the story gives speech to this view, memorably pointing out to Lewis,

> There are only two kinds of people in the end: those who say to God, "Thy will be done," and those to whom God says, in the end, "*Thy* will be done." All that are in Hell, choose it. Without that self-choice there could be no Hell. No soul that seriously and constantly desires joy will ever miss it. Those who seek find. To those who knock it is opened.[2]

In his story, Lewis is grappling with hell as a choice of human over divine will. Even if it were possible for the sinner to travel from hell to heaven, the will would not be there to complete the journey. If heaven was chosen by some means, however, the adjustment from the weightlessness and insubstantiality of hell to the painful solidity of heaven would be purgatorial. This is why hell itself, which the now solid people left behind, turns out to be purgatory rather than hell.

The idea of a purgatorial process in human salvation was much on C. S. Lewis's mind in the World War II years. His BBC radio broadcasts of that time, collected in *Mere Christianity*, are shot through with vivid images, analogies and topical references. One fine analogy, which reads as a parable, conveys Lewis's take on purgatory as a discipline preparing people for living fully human lives in heaven. He writes:

> Imagine yourself as a living house. God comes in to rebuild that house. At first, perhaps, you can understand what he is doing. He is getting the drains right and stopping the leaks in the roof and so on: you knew that those jobs needed doing and so you are not surprised. But presently he starts knocking the house about in a way that hurts abominably and does not seem to make sense. What on earth is He up to? The explanation is that He is building quite a different house from the one you thought of—throwing out a new wing here, putting on an extra floor there, running up towers, making court-yards. You thought you were going to be made into a decent little cottage: but He is building a palace. He intends to come and live in it Himself. . . .
>
> The process will be long and in parts very painful, but that is what we are in for. Nothing less.[3]

The Power of Change

The Chronicles of Narnia

The correspondence between devils in *The Screwtape Letters*, which we explored in chapter two, focuses on the individual human soul, whereas the Narnian Chronicles are somewhat more concerned with the nature of human and Christian society and the meaning of history in its peaceful and dark periods. The green and pleasant land of Narnia represents a virtuous civilization. It nevertheless features the temptations or trials of individuals, such as Eustace Scrubb, Lucy Pevensie, the young King Caspian and Jill Pole.

Narnia is a land of valleys, extending from Lantern Waste in the west to Cair Paravel on the shores of the Great Eastern Ocean. It is a pastoral, green world full of trackless woods inhabited by talking animals. Narnia has Archenland and then Calormen lying much further to its south. (Calormen is a country dominated by caste and a slavery economy, in stark contrast to the freedom enjoyed in Narnia.) Narnia is a land inhabited by both talking and dumb beasts and trees. Aslan is its creator, as well as sovereign. He is fully a talking lion and fully divine.

Narnians perceive their earth as a flat world. In *The Voyage of the Dawn Treader* Reepicheep the mouse pictures the world as having an edge. "That's how I've always imagined it," he said, "the World like a great round table and the waters of all the oceans endlessly pouring over the edge." To the north and south are territories associated with danger—the White Witch has dwelt in the north for hundreds of years, and terrifying giants live there, while far south Calormen represents a constant threat to Narnian security. Narnia is a middle world in which the qualities of ordinary life and freedom are nourished. For Aravis, in *The Horse and His Boy*, in despair over her prospects in Calormen, Narnia represents hope.[1] The storyteller always brings the implications of these threats home by featuring ordinary Narnians such as Mr. Tumnus the faun in the ruthless hands of the White Witch and the death of Roonwit the centaur by a Calormene arrow.

Narnia a "Secondary World"

For many years it was the habit of critics to look at The Chronicles of Narnia as books speedily written in a rather casual manner. The contrast is sometimes made with Tolkien, who over very many years painstakingly composed *The Lord of the Rings*, and for over half a century worked out the background world of Middle-earth. Lewis however wrote the seven Narnia stories in just seven years. Yet this rather negative comparison does not fit the actual reading experience of many, and fails to account for the power of the books. Like Tolkien, Lewis was an outstanding scholar whose specialty was the Middle Ages. His knowledge lies tangibly but unobtrusively in the stories, even though written for the level of a child. Apart from the obvious world of Narnia and its creator, Aslan, what gave the sevenfold stories their unity was a mystery, however. Attempts were made to account for what held them together so satisfactorily.

While researching the Narnian Chronicles for his doctorate, Michael Ward unearthed a feature of all the stories that he is convinced Lewis had carefully buried. Ward shows how medieval astrology, in particular, has a central role in how Lewis depicted

Narnia and the stories that play out there. He later shared his discovery in *Planet Narnia*, which has served to stimulate literary study of the Narnian stories, even for scholars cautious of the theory. *Planet Narnia* provides a marvelous insight, I believe, into the always mysterious process of making a successful "secondary world"—the feature of the imagination both Tolkien and Lewis held to be at the center of storytelling. His work in fact, to my mind, points to Lewis's creation of the world of Narnia as being as skillful in its own way and on its more limited scale as that of Tolkien's rendering of Middle-earth. Like Tolkien, Lewis drew upon the imaginative riches of the Middle Ages, allowing the vision of that period to reenchant the world of the modern reader.

Tolkien called the result of making a successful secondary world a "subcreation." This was because it is an imagined other world that is thoroughly consistent and plausible on its own inner terms. It represents human art at its best. Narnia, like Middle-earth, is indeed a subcreation. Tolkien brought into focus the storyteller's desire to have a well-imagined world for the story, in which its symbolic geography heightened and illuminated the events. Lewis's Narnia can be seen as an outstanding example of a successful secondary world, created with Tolkien's views in mind, even though, to his regret, Tolkien found himself out of sympathy with the Narnian stories. He found them too allegorical and too inconsistent in their imagery.[2] The world of Narnia itself embodies the powers of good and evil, once wrongdoing has been introduced into Narnia.

At the center of Narnia is, of course, Aslan, who is the incarnation of the divine in bodily form (in the Narnian case, embodied as a real talking lion). Lewis saw the incarnation as the central doctrine of Christian faith, brilliantly portraying it in his book *Miracles*. "Every other miracle prepares for this, or exhibits this, or results from this," writes Lewis. "Just as every natural event is the manifestation at a particular place and moment of Nature's total character, so every particular Christian miracle manifests at a particular place and moment the character and significance of the Incarnation."[3] Similarly, all events in Narnia turn out to point to Aslan, who is behind all the stories. He is in the forefront of the war between good and bad, and in him lies the secret of attaining heaven—or the New Narnia, as it is called in the stories. Hell, as it is pictured, is focused in its darkness on the demon god Tash. But some can see the original good that has been perverted in that deity who is worshiped in Calormen, such as the virtuous pagan Emeth in *The Last Battle*. Lewis also represents hell dramatically as the shadow at Aslan's left which engulfs the creatures who reject him in *The Last Battle*.

In the Chronicles there are explicit biblical parallels for those that seek them—allusions to creation, Eden, the fall of humanity and the end of the world. In one place in *The Voyage of the Dawn Treader*, the lamb offering a breakfast of fish evokes John 21 from the New Testament. There is a faithful remnant of true Narnians in *Prince Caspian*, as there was in Israel's darkest hours. The four signs given to Jill Pole in *The Silver Chair* echo the Ten Commandments or the Law.

There are many less direct references also, as, in *The Voyage of the Dawn Treader*, when Eustace casts off the dragon skin with Aslan's help or, in *The Silver Chair*, when Jill drinks from the stream in Aslan's Country. Aslan's Table, with its crimson cloth and stone knife, recalls the Eucharist and the "daily bread" promised by God. An emphasis of Lewis's in *The Screwtape Letters*, *The Great Divorce* and other books reappears throughout The Chronicles of Narnia. Small decisions that we make in life eventually fix salvation or damnation, or at least the broad direction of our likely destiny: as when Eustace slowly becomes dragonlike even before arriving at Dragon Island, or Susan little by little moves toward rejecting Narnia's reality, or Edmund declines into eventual betrayal.

The Chronicles pick up on the biblical themes of correctly seeing the world, and of evil as illusion and deception (and not an equal reality to good), which is connected with the biblical idea of idols and Satan's ability to appear as an angel of light. In the Narnian stories we find the deceptive beauty of witches like Jadis and the Green Witch (who captivates and enslaves Rilian in *The Silver Chair*). In *The Last Battle* Puzzle is dressed by Shift the ape to look like Aslan, leading to the blasphemy of Tashlan, in which the evil Tash appears to be at one with Aslan. Related to this theme of deception and illusion is the necessity of becoming undeceived and of having a radical change in perception (see chap. 10), which, in biblical terms, comes about through victory over sin and temptation. In *The Voyage of the Dawn Treader* we find the alluring spell of Deathwater broken, just in time. In *The Silver Chair* Puddleglum burns his foot in order to come to his senses (an allusion to Christ's injunction to cut out one's eye or even sacrifice one's life if necessary for the sake of truth). In *The Silver Chair* the way of escape from the giants of Harfang is a tiny cave or crack in the earth, evoking the narrow gate to life that exists for those who can see it (with the help of God's instructions).[4]

There are other Narnian moments that touch even closer to darkness in the actual world in their allusions to a biblical portrayal of reality. When Aslan confers with the White Witch in *The Lion, the Witch and the Wardrobe* over the fate of Edmund, it is a distant allusion, perhaps, to the discussion between God and Satan at the heavenly court at the beginning of the book of Job. Aslan's loneliness and the trial of his feelings before he goes to his appointment with death unmistakably recall Gethsemane. As Susan and Lucy look on the scene of Aslan's execution, the allusion seems clear: the scene is like that of the faithful women at the cross. Aslan's tears over Digory's mother are reminiscent of Christ's sorrow over Lazarus.

Underlining Lewis's stress on ways of seeing, and on perceiving properly, is the contrast through The Chronicles of Narnia in how its inhabitants see Aslan. Aslan is perceived in remarkably different ways by various characters in the stories. Indeed, in the end, how they perceive him becomes the ultimate indicator of whether they pass to his left or right, to the shadow or the light, on Narnia's Judgment Day in *The Last Battle*. That final choice, shaped by a myriad of lesser choices, is prefigured many times in the stories. The ill-fated Nikabrik, for instance, perceives Aslan as a "performing lion" in *Prince Caspian*. In *The Lion, the Witch and the Wardrobe*, the White Witch calls him the "Great Fool" before slaying him. Rabadash in *The Horse and His Boy* sees Aslan as a "demon" and a "horrible phantasm." Rather like some modern theologians, the Narnian talking horse Bree sees talk of Aslan as a lion as only figurative language (until he actually encounters him). Bree, however, is among those who are undeceived in time, suddenly seeing who Aslan really is.

One of the sharpest indicators of the theology of Narnia that was intended in some way to underlie the stories is given by Lewis himself to a child called Anne, in a letter of March 5, 1961.[5] Here Lewis explains to Anne that the whole Narnian series has foundational themes that he clearly feels will not be obvious to his child readers. In *The Magician's Nephew* there is an account of creation and how evil enters Narnia at the very beginning. In *The Lion, the Witch and the Wardrobe* is a retelling of Christ's crucifixion and resurrection appropriate to a Narnian world. *Prince Caspian* is concerned, in Lewis's words to Anne, with "restoration of true religion after a corruption." The calling and conversion of a "heathen" is the subject of *The Horse and His Boy*. *The Voyage of the Dawn Treader* portrays the spiritual life, especially in Reepicheep's quest for Aslan's Country. *The Silver Chair* particularly concerns the continuing spiritual battle against the dark powers. *The Last Battle* tells of the coming, in Shift the ape, of the antichrist, leading to the prophesied end of the world and Last Judgment.

Lewis's portrayal of the powers of goodness have nothing fragile about them. Preeminently, there is a strong element of wildness in Aslan: he is not a tame lion. As Mr. Beaver says, he isn't safe. His wildness correlates with a numinous wildness in nature, represented by figures in Narnia from pre-Christian paganism such as Bacchus and Silenus from classical mythology and giants from northern and Celtic legend. Lewis balances Aslan's wildness and at times terrifying nature perfectly with his approachability, beauty and gentleness. In *The Lion, the Witch and the Wardrobe*, we are told, Lucy and Susan do something they would never have dared to do without Aslan's permission: they sink their cold hands into the sea of his beautiful mane to comfort him. After his resurrection, he romps with them, and Lucy afterwards can't make up her mind whether it was like dancing with a thunderstorm or with a kitten. As for his awesomeness, Aslan's roar is magnificently portrayed in *Prince Caspian*: "The sound, deep and throbbing at first like an organ beginning on a low note, rose and became louder, and then far louder again, till the earth and air were shaking with it. It rose up from that hill and floated across all Narnia."[6]

Not only in his wildness does Aslan have a spiritual quality. It is evident in other ways also, expressing the attractiveness of sheer goodness. The very mention of his name stirs the children deeply in *The Lion, the Witch and the Wardrobe*, even before they have met him. His numinous quality is associated with his scent, with music and with light. For Susan, his very name evokes a delicious smell or a delightful strain of distant music. When Shasta in *The Horse and His Boy* falls at the feet of the unknown lion, a strange and solemn perfume that hangs about the mane envelops him. As the voyagers in *The Voyage of the Dawn Treader* approach Aslan's Country at the end of the world, the quality of light takes on a new dimension. It would be too bright to bear but for the strange, strengthening power of the sweet seawater they drink. In that light they can glimpse features of a blissful, heavenly country.

All seven of the Chronicles are astir with hidden meanings whose secrets are unlocked in other writings of Lewis's, such as the true character of God and the nature of humanity, the natural world, the influence on our lives now of heaven and hell, and, as his signature theme, joy (the deep longing to which his autobiography, *Surprised by Joy*, was devoted). The key to these meanings lies in the fact that Aslan is a rendering of Christ, supposing that there is a land of talking animals in which he became incarnate as a talking lion. If a reader is unaware of this, he or she can still enjoy the stories in their own right; if he or she is aware, the meaning of Christian truths often comes strangely alive. Many readers are moved to tears for instance at the death of Aslan though they may be so familiar with the Gospel narratives as to be unmoved by the accounts of Christ's death. The imaginative power of these meanings is drawn from Lewis's hallmark vision of reality, which was nourished for him by his knowledge of thought and imagination in the Middle Ages, and the rich classical and pagan worlds that preceded that epoch.

The meanings that Lewis built into the world and stories of Narnia derived not only from his Christian beliefs. He felt that all human beings had them in unfocused and often unapprehended form. The memory of them was carried in persistent patterns in stories and indeed in the languages we use. The meanings may range from a knowledge of right and wrong in what we call conscience to glimpses of God himself through the real world in which we live. Glimpses of God may come in direct experience of him, even if he is unknown to us or if we deny his existence. In the Narnian stories, there is much about forgotten or dimly glimpsed knowledge. Lewis even borrows images from the ancient Greek and pagan philosopher Plato to depict the present world of Narnia as the Shadowlands, whose full glory and light is revealed in *The Last Battle*.

Amnesia and Lost and Distant Knowledge

Amnesia and partly apprehended knowledge is in fact a plot device common in fantasy literature, whether it is a spell representing bondage through forgetting or the absence of important knowledge. In *The Silver Chair*, Prince Rilian is kept in a state of amnesia about

Narnia and his true status as a Narnian prince, only coming out of his forgetfulness once a day, when he is bound to a silver chair to stop him acting on his knowledge. In *The Horse and His Boy*, Shasta is unaware that he is anything more than an ordinary Calormene boy, though he knows he is an orphan and that his skin color is different from other Calormenes. He senses that he lacks some important knowledge about himself.

In the Wood Between the Worlds in *The Magician's Nephew*, a borderland of many portals to various worlds, arriving travelers very quickly fall into a state of pleasant stupor and forgetfulness, although the wicked witch Jadis finds it a place of terror, particularly as her strength fails. In the wood, life becomes like something in a dream, where visitors are in danger of sleeping forever. In *The Voyage of the Dawn Treader*, in contrast, forgetfulness of sleep is a blessing for Lord Rhoop after his experiences on the Dark Island, a place where nightmares come true.

In *The Silver Chair*, the later Green Witch uses a weapon of amnesia or forgetfulness not only on Prince Rilian but, in a different way, on the gnomes in Underland. This was originally a happy place. She brings Underlanders from the deep realm of Bism to a region nearer the world's surface, where they work for her in glum servitude, their memory of their past hidden from them by her enchantment.

C. S. Lewis did not only employ stories to bring us out of forgetfulness into a state of wakefulness. He believed that our experiences in everyday living are pointers to how to live. There are signposts helping us to know whether our way is taking us imperceptibly toward goodness or evil, toward heaven or hell. Some of the most telling clues, he believed, lay in our deepest affections and in human love itself, of which affection is a part.

Pain and Love

The Four Loves, Till We Have Faces and A Grief Observed

There is much in C. S. Lewis's writings, including his letters, about ordinary human life, and ordinary human loves in particular. He always saw human trials and dilemmas in the larger, supernatural context of spiritual powers of good and of evil. Though these powers were not pitted in an eternal battle, the cosmic conflict was for him very real. The struggles of human beings to live right and to love right, no matter how ordinary the plane of the drama, involved for him not only our inner lives but forces external to us that were part of nature in its widest sense. They were part of the character and texture of reality, which for him was a nature of many dimensions, not merely those perceptible through our physical senses. His book *The Four Loves* sets out a simple anatomy of human love. *Till We Have Faces*, novel composed late in his life, is a fresh exploration of human suffering, pain and love written in some collaboration at least with Joy Davidman, the American poet and novelist he was to marry. His *A Grief Observed*, written immediately after Joy's death from cancer after a period of happy remission, revealed a deepening, but not a contradiction, of Lewis's much earlier reflections on pain and evil.

Lewis once remarked that hell is the only place outside of heaven "where you can be perfectly safe from all the dangers . . . of love."[1] He situated human love within the mystery and infinity of divine love. In trying to distinguish different kinds of love he drew heavily on his knowledge of classics for the help he could find there. Especially, he spotlighted four loves that have their own distinct Greek names. Like Tolkien and another close friend, Owen Barfield, Lewis was very aware of the depth of meaning carried in words and names— embodying religious, mythological, philosophical, scientific and very ordinary human wisdom. His outline of the meaning of human love, and its vulnerability in the conflict of goodness and badness, takes us into his treatment of the intense human pain and suffering that love makes possible.

The Four Loves

The four loves of this title of a book by Lewis are set out as affection, friendship, erotic love (eros), and charity (divine love). The respective Greek words that he expounds are *storge*, *philia*, *eros* and *agape*. This anatomy of love was written by Lewis during his brief but happy marriage to Joy Davidman. He shows how each love is able to overlap into another or even take on the quality of another. He believes it is vital however not to miss out on the real differences that give each love its valid character.

Lewis reasons that "we must join neither the idolaters nor the 'debunkers' of human love. . . . Our loves do not make their claim to divinity until the claim becomes plausible. It does not become plausible until there is in them a real resemblance to God, to Love Himself."[2]

Affection is the humblest and most widely spread of the four loves. Most of whatever real and consistent happiness we find in our lives can be put down to affection. It is not a particularly appreciative love. This very lack of close attention gives it the scope to broaden the mind and to create a feeling for other people of all shapes and sizes. Lewis liked an observation he once came across: "Dogs and cats should always be brought up together. It broadens their minds so." Affection penetrates the whole texture of our lives. It is a need love. Lewis observes, "In ordinary life no one calls a child selfish because it turns for comfort to its mother; nor an adult who turns to his fellow 'for company.'"[3]

Lewis explored the virtues and dangers of affection in much of his fiction. In *The Great Divorce*, which we looked at earlier, the ghost of a mother still desires to control her son after death. In the novel *Till We Have Faces* the deep affection Orual feels for her sister Psyche turns into a destructive jealousy that she cannot distinguish from love (see more later).

Friendship, for Lewis, is the least instinctive and necessary of our loves. Even today it is hardly considered a love, and Lewis was unusual among his contemporaries in devoting so much of his attention to this theme. Lewis complained that "very few modern people think Friendship . . . a love at all."[4] Lewis points out that the ancients put the highest value on this love, as in the friendship between David and Jonathan. The ideal climate for friendship, believed Lewis, is when a few people are absorbed in some shared interest. Lovers are usually imagined face to face; friends are best imagined side by side, their eyes ahead on their common interest.

Friendship was deeply important to Lewis throughout his life. Arthur Greeves was a lifelong friend, as was Owen Barfield. Friendship formed the basis of the association of the Inklings. In Joy Davidman he found a friend who became his wife. He had other female friendships too, including Sister Penelope, Dorothy L. Sayers and the poet Ruth Pitter. Friendship, reckoned Lewis, made good people better and bad people worse. Sharing a disinterested point of view was not itself good enough for ensuring that friendships help in living a life that is marked by goodness.

Eros is the kind of love that lovers are within or "in"—the state of being in love. It is different from mere physical, sexual desire in that eros primarily wants the beloved, not sex as an end in itself. In eros love, people are taken out of themselves and thus are enlarged as persons. Eros would value the beloved above happiness and pleasure, and would wish to retain the beloved even if the result was unhappiness. Lewis characteristically felt that, were we not human beings, we should find eros hard to imagine. As it is, we find it difficult to explain.

The fourth love, charity, or divine, agape love, rises above all earthly loves in being a gift love. All human loves, believed Lewis, are by nature need loves. If we are in fact created beings, we, by necessity, have to turn to God for our fulfillment and meaning, Lewis saw this pattern repeated throughout creation, in our dependence as human beings on other people and on nature. Our human loves, he warned, are potential rivals to the love of God, and can only take their proper place if our first allegiance is to him. All of God's love for us and for his creation is gift love, Lewis argued, as he has no need of the universe and its inhabitants for his existence and fulfillment.

As with several other of his books of popular Christian theology, Lewis concludes by looking to heaven as the ultimate context of human life. The divine likeness in all our human loves is their heavenly and thus permanent element. Only what is heaven-like can eventually enter heaven; all else, when shaken, will fall. Thus any love for someone or something that is allowed to be a proper love has a heavenly element and is, in fact, also a love for God. When those that enter heaven see God, they will find that they know him already.

Till We Have Faces: A Myth Retold

Till We Have Faces, published in 1956, was written with help from the novelist and poet Joy Davidman, whom Lewis married that year. The book is dedicated to her. In it he retells an ancient myth, that of Cupid and Psyche, one that had haunted him for very many years. Joy

Davidman helped him to realize it as a novel—his only work of fiction written within the perspective of the first person that is also female.

Lewis took the myth from Apuleius's second century *The Golden Ass*. In Apuleius's story, Psyche is so beautiful that Venus becomes jealous of her. Cupid, sent by Venus to make Psyche fall in love with an ugly creature, himself falls in love with her. After bringing her to a palace, he only visited her in the dark and forbade her to see his face. Out of jealousy, Psyche's sisters told her that her lover was a monster who would devour her. She took a lamp one night and looked at Cupid's face, but a drop of oil awoke him. In anger, the god left her. Psyche sought her lover throughout the world. Venus set her to various impossible tasks, all of which she accomplished except the last, when curiosity made her open a deadly casket from the underworld. At last, however, she was allowed to marry Cupid.

In *Till We Have Faces*, Lewis essentially follows the classical myth, but retells it through the eyes of Queen Orual, Psyche's sister, who seeks to defend her actions to the gods as being the result of deep love for Psyche, not jealousy. Lewis casts the myth in the realistic setting of a historical novel. It is set several hundred years before Christ in the imaginary and barbaric country of Glome, somewhere to the north of the Greeklands.

Having heard a legend in the nearby land of Essur similar to this myth of Cupid and Psyche, Queen Orual seeks to correct the record. The gods, she claims, have distorted the story in certain vital respects. She recognizes herself and her half-sister Psyche in the newly sprung up legend.

The gods, she said, had called her deep love for Psyche jealousy. They had also said that she saw Psyche's palace, whereas Orual had only seen shapes in a mist, a fantasy that momentarily resembled a palace. There had been no evidence that Psyche had married a god and dwelt in his palace. Orual therefore tells her version of the story, being as truthful as possible. She had a reader in mind from the

Greeklands and agreed with the Greek demand for truth and rational honesty. She has to recount her life story to do this properly.

Early in the story, Orual is a princess, the daughter of a barbarian and callous king, Trom, and has a sister, Redival. Orual's mother had died young, so Trom marries again and the stepmother dies giving birth to the beautiful Psyche. Psyche's outstanding beauty contrasts with Orual's ugliness (in later life she wore a veil—hence the reference in the book's title to not having a face). The king engages a Greek slave, nicknamed "The Fox," to teach his daughters. The Fox is able to pass on his Greek Stoicism and rationalism to Orual.

In Glome the goddess Ungit, a deformed version of Venus, is worshiped. After a drought and other disasters a lot falls on the innocent Psyche to be sacrificed on the Grey Mountains to the Shadowbrute or West-wind, the god of the mountain.

Sometime afterwards, Orual, accompanied by a faithful member of the king's guard, Bardia, seeks the bones of Psyche to bury her. Finding no trace of Psyche, Bardia and Orual explore further and find the beautiful and sheltered valley of the god. Here Psyche is living, wearing rags but full of health. She claims to be married to the god of the mountain, whose face she has never seen. Orual, afraid that the "god" is a monster or outlaw, persuades Psyche, against her will, to shine a light on her husband's face, while sleeping. As in the Greek myth, Psyche as a result is condemned to wander the earth, doing impossible tasks. In the terrible storm, which disfigures the valley, Orual seems to see a beautiful god who tells her, "You also shall be Psyche."

Queen Orual's account goes on to record the bitter years of her suffering and grief at the loss of Psyche, haunted because she can hear Psyche's weeping. Succeeding King Trom, she reforms the kingdom and does her best to rule justly, applying civilized principles learned via The Fox from the Greeks. She becomes a great queen and a renowned warrior. Late in life she decides to travel the wider world and it is then she hears what she believes to be the warped story of Orual, Psyche and the god, causing her to write her account. Most of *Till We Have Faces* is made up of this narration.

The short second part of the novel—still in Orual's voice—continues a few days later. Orual has undergone a devastating release from her self-deception, whereby, in painful self-knowledge, she discovers how her affection for Psyche had become poisoned by possessiveness. She is eventually able to say to Psyche, "Never again will I call you mine, but all there is of me shall be yours." Her clinging and impossible love for Bardia had also blighted his life. She had also dominated the life of her servant, The Fox. In these recognitions, which allowed the restoration of a true love for Psyche, was the consolation that she had also been Psyche, as the god had said. She had suffered on Psyche's behalf, in a substitutionary manner, bearing her burdens and thus easing her tasks. By what Charles Williams called "the Way of Exchange," Orual had thus helped Psyche to be reunited with her divine husband. With the curing of her poisoned and obsessive love, Orual in a vision sees that she has become herself beautiful. She has gained a face in becoming a full person. After this reconciliation, the aged queen Orual dies, her narration ending with her.

Till We Have Faces is unlike Lewis's other fiction and is consequently less easy to interpret. It in fact repays several readings. One key to the novel (it has several rich layers of meaning) is the theme of love, which Lewis, as we saw, expounded in his *The Four Loves*. The loves of affection and eros are particularly explored, but friendship and agape (divine or gift love) are also skillfully woven into the novel. Orual's crippling self-centeredness takes the form of possessive love, distorting what it should have been. Only as she steps out of the prison of her selfish obsessions is Orual able to be truly herself and truly able to love her sister. She is also able to see past distorted images to the beauty of God, the vision Psyche had followed. The critic Charles Hutter aptly highlights the theme of identity in the novel:

Orual's lack of self-knowledge, her self-deception, is embodied in the veil she wears much of her life. The veil gives her an identity as the Queen, but allows her to bury her personal self and establishes a barrier between herself and others, and herself and the divine. She has no face, no identity, and thus has no way to relate to the divine. Only when she removes the veil, confronts her true self, and gains a "face" can she encounter God face-to-face, without defenses, excuses, or pretenses. Only then can she attain an authentic relationship with God, with others, and with herself.[5]

Till We Have Faces has several affinities with the British novelist William Golding's *The Double Tongue*, published after his death in 1995. Lewis's novel does not suffer in the comparison with this great writer. Both use a first-person perspective, and both adopt for the first time the voice of a female narrator. The narrators, Orual and Arieka, in Golding's story, are elderly when they write, looking back over their lives in the classical world before Christ. Each has a dramatic encounter with spiritual forces that results in a twist in the story at or near the end. Both women are plain-faced. Orual adopts a veil, which she wears constantly, while Arieka often puts one on. Orual's self-deception is shattered when she sees the beauty and love of the god she thought ugly and banally cruel. Arieka struggles in her belief in the gods like Apollo who turn their backs on her, but encounters an unknown god in the void in which "there was a kind of tenderness"— her long life as the servant of the oracle at Delphi turns out not to be meaningless, despite the deceits she hates that have taken place there.

Being "Undeceived"
There are moments of sudden recognition in our lives that result in a new perception of events, and perhaps even of reality itself. Such moments can be what Lewis called occasions of "undeception." He

borrowed this quality from a favorite novelist, Jane Austen. The shattering of Orual's self-centeredness, and the change from possessive to wholesome love, is perhaps Lewis's most sustained treatment of undeception. In his stories, the way out of the self and toward heaven almost always requires some such recognition. His hope is that in some way the reader also will undergo some change of perception for the better. Chad Walsh points out how much Lewis's style facilitates looking through his words to reality outside and beyond. Walsh calls Lewis's style "flexible and gracious."

> It is straight to the point, lean, free of inflated language and the technical jargon of the professions. At the same time, thanks particularly to the use of exact metaphors, it is capable of modulating into highly poetic effects—more poetic, in fact, than most of Lewis's verse. It is a modest style, summoning the reader to go beyond the exact words and to retain in his memory not the words but what they point to.[6]

"Undeception" was a favorite theme of C. S. Lewis, for whom a characteristic of the human condition is the state of being deceived by others, by sin or by oneself. *The Screwtape Letters*, of course, masterfully explores the subtleties of deceit practiced by Wormwood, with Screwtape's help, on the young man, the "Patient." Lewis refers to the concept of "undeception" in his essay "A Note on Jane Austen," in *Selected Literary Essays*, finding the theme in her novels. Many of Lewis's fictional characters come to recognize that they have been deceived, often but not always associated with salvation. Many times it involves stepping outside of self-deception, however painful this is. Such characters experiencing undeception include Mark Studdock in *That Hideous Strength*, Elwin Ransom in *Out of the Silent Planet* (which frees him from fear), and Queen Orual in *Till We Have Faces*. In Lewis's first fiction, *The Pilgrim's Regress*, John undergoes many undeceptions about the nature of joy (as Lewis himself did, as recounted in his autobiography, *Surprised by Joy*). John, for instance, confuses a desire for the island with sexual lust.

Lewis regarded one purpose of his fiction as helping to undeceive his contemporaries, whom he regarded as separated from the past, with its knowledge of perennial human values, and from an acquaintance with even basic Christian teaching about the realities of sin, redemption, immortality, divine judgment and grace. Where there was some knowledge of Christian tradition, it had "stained-glass and Sunday School associations," Lewis said. In one place, he described the subversive process of undeceiving as stealing "past those watchful dragons,"[7] and "watchful dragons" is a phrase that could apply to all that deceives human beings and keeps us from truly seeing. Fantasy is a perfect mode for subverting false perception. Lewis spoke of George MacDonald's *Phantastes* "baptizing" his imagination and, like MacDonald, many of his best writings are fantasy.

Undeception is an instance of a quality of *recognition* in Lewis's fiction—a quality that has theological implications. According to the *Encyclopedia of Fantasy*, recognition affirms a story-shaped world. For Aristotle, "Recognition marks a fundamental shift in the process of a story from increasing ignorance to knowledge."[8] Protagonists, in a sense, recognize that they are in a story—a narrative structure precedes the event they are in and will reach a conclusion subsequent to that event.

For Lewis, and also for Tolkien, the supreme pattern for stories is inherent in the Gospel narratives. Prefigurations of the supreme story in human myths helped Tolkien to convince Lewis of the truth of Christ's claims, sometime after his move from atheism, via various inns on the road, to theism—to belief in a personal deity. A key moment of recognition in the Gospels is Christ's resurrection—the sudden turn that denies final defeat. Lewis memorably captures this turn in the restoration of Aslan after his cruel death on the

Stone Table. This was in his first Narnia story, written in the immediate postwar period, which picked up mental pictures and ideas that came to Lewis during two wartimes.

"A Grief Observed"

A Grief Observed is one of the last books that C. S. Lewis wrote. It expounds his long-held insight that it is when we love that we feel pain in our relationships. To understand the book's significance fully, it is necessary to look a little at the late love of Lewis's life, Helen Joy Davidman (1915–1960). Joy was Lewis's wife and the subject of his book. Her son of her first marriage, Douglas, notes that its title refers to "a grief," rather than grief in general, that is observed.[9] It was a particular grief that he observed in two senses: to attend to, go through and comply with, and also to reflect and meditate on. *A Grief Observed* was written after Joy's death from cancer at the age of forty-five. Joy Davidman was a poet and novelist from a New York Jewish family, and she also published a study of the Ten Commandments, *Smoke on the Mountain*. Lewis's attraction to her was at first merely intellectual, that of friendship, though Joy found herself deeply in love with Lewis. She was at that time on the verge of divorce, with two young sons. Joy had been converted to Christianity from Marxism partly through reading Lewis's books.

A short time after meeting Lewis in England, Joy Davidman came to live in Oxford with her sons. She and Lewis became on close terms. In retrospect he wrote, "Her mind was lithe and quick and muscular as a leopard. Passion, tenderness and pain were all equally unable to disarm it. It scented the first whiff of cant or slush; then sprang, and knocked you over before you knew what was happening."[10] They eventually married in a civil ceremony in April 1956, with the sole intention, on Lewis's part, of giving her and her sons British nationality.

In the autumn of that year they learned that Joy had terminal cancer. It was sudden, unexpected news, and Lewis was deeply shocked. Cancer was an old acquaintance. Her two boys were about the same age as the Lewis brothers had been when their mother died; the parallels were uncomfortable. Lewis had to act, not least because his feelings toward Joy had changed in the face of death. He reached out to her needs as long before he had reached out to Mrs. Moore. A bedside Christian wedding ceremony took place on March 21, 1957. Joy came home to The Kilns, Lewis's home, to die.

After prayer for healing, Joy had an unexpected reprieve. Her horridly diseased bones rejuvenated against all medical expectations and by July that year she was well enough to get out and about. The next year Joy and Lewis had a fortnight's vacation in Ireland, and others followed. The remission was the beginning of the happiest few years of both their lives. Lewis confessed to fellow Inkling Nevill Coghill, "I never expected to have, in my sixties, the happiness that passed me by in my twenties."[11]

Lewis's brother, Warnie, points out that the marriage fulfilled "a whole dimension to his nature that had previously been starved and thwarted."[12] It also put to rest a bachelor's doubt that God was an invented substitute for love. "For those few years H. and I feasted on love," Lewis recalled in *A Grief Observed*, "every mode of it— solemn and merry, romantic and realistic, sometimes as dramatic as a thunderstorm, sometimes as comfortable and unemphatic as putting on your soft slippers."[13]

The cancer eventually returned, but the Lewises were able to have a trip to Greece in the spring of the year of her death, a journey much desired by both of them. They were accompanied by the writer Roger Lancelyn Green and his wife, June. The story of the happiness that had come to Lewis so late in life, and subsequent bitter bereavement, has been made into two successful films and a play based around a similar script by William Nicolson, titled *Shadowlands.* The dramatic license used in all versions has created much debate, but they each are extraordinarily poignant. Many in their audiences have been inspired to read Lewis for the first time.

A Grief Observed

"No one ever told me grief felt so like fear."[14]

This is the book's memorable first line. Originally published under a pseudonym, N. W. Clerk, because of its personal nature, this slim book sets out C. S. Lewis's pilgrimage through bereavement after losing Joy Davidman. Some people sent him the book by "N. W. Clerk," thinking it might bring comfort in his grief!

A Grief Observed complements his study The Problem of Pain. He wrote it as a kind of journal of grief. Whereas The Problem of Pain explores suffering generally and theoretically, the journal observes it specifically and personally, through lived experience. Like the earlier book, A Grief Observed affirms the presence of God in the deepest human darkness, even when he for long seems absent. Biographically, A Grief Observed reveals the quality of relationship between Lewis and Joy Davidman. He remembers, "She was my daughter and my mother, my pupil and my teacher, my subject and my sovereign; and always, holding all these in solution, my trusty comrade, friend, shipmate, fellow-soldier."[15] Many will agree with Denise Imwold, who wrote that the book "is arguably one of the finest meditations on death and mourning written in modern English literature. Written in the elegant, balanced prose style of a master, it supports the sentiment expressed in Shadowlands: 'We read to know we're not alone.'"[16]

Lewis's raw but beautiful prose falls into parts. The first dwells on the immediate pain of his loss. When he tries to turn to God for comfort, it feels as if a door has been slammed in his face. Whether he wonders about Joy's continued existence after death, or asks where God is now, there is always no answer. Wherever he turns, there is silence. In the second part, Lewis begins to face up to the self-absorption of grief, the total attention that pain demands of us.

He reasons more, but finds no comfort in the thought that Joy is in God's hands. He finds that it is difficult not to say, "God forgive God." Then he thinks, "But if our faith is true, He didn't. He crucified him."[17] He eventually returns to his long-held belief that our judgment that God is evil doesn't and cannot make sense. In the third part of the book, Lewis examines his own faith and its inadequacy in the observance of grief. Did this mean that it was empty? He starts to discover that he has been through a process in which he has begun to accept God's hand in the loss. Loving someone has to mean pain in parting from them. He says, "I find I now can believe again."[18] The final part has the realization that when he now turns to God, he no longer meets a locked door. Indeed, it is unlikely it was ever slammed in his face. He finds comfort in the future resurrection of the body, rather than in speculating about the state that Joy is in now that she is with God. A little over three weeks after Joy's death, in a letter to one of his long-term correspondents, a Mrs. Vera Gebbert (formerly, Mathews), he writes, "I believe in the resurrection, and also (rather less confidently) in the natural immortality of the soul. But the state of the dead *till* the resurrection is unimaginable. Are they in the same *time* that we live in at all. And if not, is there any sense in asking what they are 'now'?"[19] Grief, Lewis finds, is a process rather than state, a mappable journey he had to go through, in all its anguish. By the end, he had been through "all the hells of young grief."[20]

Lewis summed up his book in starkest terms to a correspondent, Sister Madeleva, a few weeks before he died: "It is 'a grief *observed*' from day to day in all its rawness and sinful reactions and follies. It ends with faith but raises all the blackest doubts *en route*." Nevertheless, he arranged for his publisher, Faber, to send her copy.[21]

The poetic quality of Lewis's prose in his record of a grief is part of his resolution of the sorrow. The writing helps him to be lifted up above his specific and tangible pain to the universal quality of grief, without losing the book's focus on a real, individual person whom he had lost. Poetry can hold together the individual and the generalization in the way that abstract thought always struggles to achieve. Lewis's distinct mark as a writer of both fiction and non-fiction is his poetic way of seeing, which was fulfilled by and central to his convictions as a Christian.

This sensibility is most present in his prose fiction, but also was part of the attractiveness of his teaching style, whether writing literary history and criticism or popular philosophical theology. For him great stories and myth have, like poetry, the ability to make general ideas like love, bereavement, courage and self-sacrifice tangible, specific and individual. In fact such stories, he felt, can give us as readers actual sensations and feelings that we may never before have experienced (like being in battle or walking on Mars). Lewis's poetic way of seeing is found, for instance, in The Chronicles of Narnia, *The Pilgrim's Regress, Till We Have Faces, Out of the Silent Planet* and *Perelandra*. Don W. King argues that it is also to be found in nonfiction books like his *A Grief Observed.*

A poetic sensibility is fundamental to Lewis's writings, as he once revealed in a letter: "The imaginative man in me is older, more continuously operative, and in that sense more basic than either the religious writer or the critic."[22]

The distinguished poet Ruth Pitter became a friend of Lewis, and, though admiring some of his verse, recognized that his true poetry resided in his poetic prose, especially in his fiction. It is into prose that Lewis most found expression for his "poetic impulse," as Don W. King calls it. There is also, however, poetic prose embedded in his books of teaching, such as essays and popular theology like *The Problem of Pain, Miracles, A Grief Observed* and *Letters to Malcolm.* King, in a major study of Lewis, the poet, believes:

> In *A Grief Observed*, Lewis works through his grief . . . to a new understanding and a renewed faith; it is his free verse

lament for Joy, himself, and his understanding of God.

Perelandra and *A Grief Observed* suggest Lewis's propensity toward poetic prose. Other of Lewis's prose works, including *Mere Christianity*, *The Problem of Pain*, *The Screwtape Letters*, *The Great Divorce*, *The Chronicles of Narnia*, as well as others, demonstrate similar poetic elements, though not as extended nor marked as these.[23]

There is poetic thought throughout the final paragraph of the second part of *A Grief Observed*. "H" is "Helen" (i.e., Helen Joy Davidman), one of the great losses of his life.

One flesh. Or, if you prefer, one ship. The starboard engine has gone. I, the port engine, must chug along somehow till we make harbour. Or rather, till the journey ends. How can I assume a harbour? A lee shore, more likely, a black night, a deafening gale, breakers ahead—and any lights shown from the land probably being waved by wreckers. Such was H's landfall. Such was my mother's. I say their landfalls; not their arrivals.[24]

Release from Hell's Snares

Lewis and the Road Out of the Self to Gain the Self

A t the heart of C. S. Lewis's exploration of the impact of the powers of heaven and hell, evil and suffering, happiness and misery—taken up in many wartime writings—is the question of the human self. Lewis believed firmly in the reality of the self. When a person uses "I" or "me" in a sentence, he or she is referring to a real self and not to some illusion projected by our brains which we mistake for a reality. When Lewis writes about human existence after death, even in the imaginative form of stories like *The Screwtape Letters* or *The Great Divorce*, he is not talking about a double illusion—an imaginary self that supposedly survives the death of the body. He memorably writes, "There are no *ordinary* people. You have never talked to a mere mortal. Nations, cultures, arts, civilisations—these are mortal, and their life is to ours as the life of a gnat. But it is immortals whom we joke with, work with, marry, snub, and exploit—immortal horrors or everlasting splendours."[1] This view of the glory or degradation of the so-called ordinary person is at the very heart of his vision of reality.

The root of understanding the path toward hell or heaven, for Lewis, is not speculation about what people experience in the afterlife (as in Emanuel Swedenborg's influential *Heaven and Hell*, published in 1758). Rather, the secret lies in the self. In one path we put our self at the center of all things, clinging to it; in the other we lay down our selves (with God's help), and in this surrender and death only do we find ourselves. In the process of persuading his readers to find heaven rather than hell, Lewis seeks a road out of the self. Here he follows the footprints of his own path to God from atheism to theism ("probably the most reluctant convert in England") and then to a belief in Jesus Christ. At the heart of his modern-day pilgrimage to belief was the unquenchable longing, or "Joy," that we shall explore in chapter twelve. After his conversion he could write, "I now know that the experience [of Joy], considered as a state of my own mind, had never had the kind of importance I once gave it. It was valuable only as a pointer to something other and outer."[2]

Lewis considers the self in many writings. In *The Screwtape Letters*, for instance, Uncle Screwtape's advice to his nephew Wormwood is to keep his Patient's attention focused on the self and away from God.[3] Here is a flavor of his insights from various writings:

> The turning from God to self . . . is a sin possible even to Paradisal man, because the mere existence of a self—the mere fact that we call it "me"—includes, from the first, the danger of self-idolatry.[4]

> From the highest to the lowest, self exists to be abdicated and, by that abdication, becomes the more truly self, to be thereupon yet the more abdicated, and so forever. . . . What is outside the system of self-giving is not earth, nor nature, or "ordinary life," but simply and solely Hell.[5]

> It is better to love the self than to love nothing and to pity the self than to pity no one.[6]

The instrument through which you see God is your whole self.
. . . And if a man's self is not kept clean and bright, his glimpse
of God will be blurred.[7]

The moment you have a self at all, there is a possibility of
putting yourself first—wanting to be the centre—wanting to
be God. That was the sin of Satan.[8]

The New Testament has lots to say about self-denial, but not
about self-denial as an end in itself.[9]

Surprisingly, Lewis's preoccupation with self-sacrifice, and (in a
phrase that now seems old-fashioned) "self-denial," now actually is
even more topical today than when he was writing. In 1979, a decade
and a half after Lewis's death, the historian Christopher Lasch published a groundbreaking study that adapted what was known as an
individual personality disorder to understand a new trend characteristic of modern American society. People, he argued, were increasingly
displaying a weakened sense of self that required constant bolstering.

In the ancient myth of Narcissus, a young man falls in love with his
own reflection. Hence the use of the term *narcissism* to denote a kind
of self-absorption. Lasch in his study put his central idea like this:

The irrational terror of old age and death is closely associated
with the emergence of the narcissistic personality. . . . Because
the narcissist has so few inner resources, he looks to others to
validate his sense of self. He needs to be admired for his beauty,
charm, celebrity, or power—attributes that usually fade with
time. Unable to achieve satisfying sublimations in the form of
love and work, he finds that he has little to sustain him when
youth passes him by. He takes no interest in the future.[10]

Here I'm not so much interested in the accuracy of Lasch's analysis,
or of psychological theories about narcissism in individuals, as in a

growing uncertainty about the self and self-identity in modern society which reflects wider worldviews. These might be secular (where a materialist view of human beings claims to abolish a reasoned view that the self is real) or religious (where beliefs might pander to personal comfort "zones" and self-absorption). For some people, personal significance and human meaning can be at best only a useful fantasy providing social bonds. For others, God or a guiding mind provides both a sense of self identity and authority for it.[11]

Many of the books by C. S. Lewis that we have looked at are fantasies—works that appeal to the imagination. Does this mean that they are not valid for the times when we actually reason about the self rather than imagine it? Could they be no more than the fantasy of a self, as in secularism, that is useful in building community and society? Unlike secularism, however, Lewis argues that we can think clearly about an actual self and how you and I relate to the real world using ideas from classical and more recent thinkers, and from the Christian or sometimes other religious tradition. When we do this, we can reach the same conclusion (and essentially point to the same vision) that we gain when our perception is shaped by stories like *Perelandra*, *The Screwtape Letters* and *The Great Divorce*. For the secularist, however, materialist reasoning about the world must cause the concept of a real self to evaporate. Such a conclusion is built into its very assumptions.

Lewis did not undertake any analysis of narcissism as such either in the individual or as a social trend. What he did do was to focus on the activity of the self, based on some thorough thinking about the character of human freedom in a world that has a very definite and resistant nature.[12] This is a real environment in which the self is located and that can be studied by the sciences as well as painted and written and sung about by the human arts. When he writes about egoism, or simply an individual's wish to do his own will instead of God's, what he concludes is worth considering as a key to understanding what is right and wrong about our human situation. We can see that theories of narcissism can cast light upon social trends that affect us all (as in Christopher Lasch's book). Lewis's exploration of the self, I believe, helps us similarly to see our situation in a fresh way (and with some resemblances to an analysis of narcissism). He intends to suggest a road out of the self, which paradoxically leads to the saving of the self, which follows from his picture of the dramatic impact of self-centeredness and rampant egoism. This intention can be seen in a number of his books from the wartime period, but the concern is evident in his writings from *The Pilgrim's Regress* in 1933 onward. Just as we should have compassion on a narcissistic person doubting his or her identity and self-worth, Lewis writes with understanding of and empathy for people fused into self-will or into a way of seeing that locks them in themselves—as when he portrays vignettes of people struggling with their self-centeredness in *The Great Divorce*, his fantasy about hell and heaven, and a surprising excursion from one to the other.

For Lewis, affection gone wrong can be a particularly painful example of self-centeredness. As we saw in chapters eight and ten, he explored the importance and also snares of affection in his writings, from a mother who still desires to assert a hold over her son after death to a queen whose very real affection for her sister turns into a life-changing jealousy.

Self-will and Suffering

The many ways that suggest a road out of the self in Lewis's writings reflect both his complexity and the central place that self-knowledge had in his concerns. In the war between the powers of good and evil in the universe he posits many strategies used by both sides— one to ensnare the self and the other to help to liberate it. In *The Great Divorce*, as we saw, the Solid People try to reason with wraithlike visitors from hell, to open their eyes to the only possible human fulfillment in heaven. In *Till We Have Faces* the sudden removal of Orual's self-deception allows her to achieve human bliss and to be reunited with her beloved sister, Psyche. At the end Psyche says, "Did I not tell you, Maia [Orual] . . . that a day was coming when you and I would meet in my house and no cloud between us?" Orual's response is, "Joy silenced me. And I thought I had now come to the highest, and to the utmost fullness of being which the human soul can contain."[13] Much of Orual's life had been spent in pain, mostly especially in the loss of her sister at her hand. In retrospect, perhaps, her life could be seen as purgatorial in the light of its happy ending.

Pain is an issue that preoccupied Lewis much at the outbreak of a second war. In 1939 he did not know that it would become a world war, but he had no illusions about its meaning. In 1940 he published *The Problem of Pain* (see chap. 5), and in it pain is not only seen in its negative form, in the issue of why people suffer, but also positively as another road out of the self. Lewis devotes two chapters to the theme of human pain.

As part of what he explores in these chapters (there is much more to what he says), he considers that very much of the suffering in the world is born out the wickedness of those who have abused their freedom of will. It is so difficult to abandon self-will that such an act of surrender might be considered a kind of death. Might not pain be one of God's ways of helping someone to confront his or her self-will and make its destruction possible before that very self-will destroys the person? Lewis memorably writes, "God whispers to us in our pleasures, speaks in our conscience, but shouts in our pains: it is His megaphone to rouse a deaf world."[14] It is because self-will is so entrenched in us that God has to be so *pain*staking in leading us out of ourselves in order that our selves may live. We need pain as a remedy and a corrective in order to help us to surrender and to allow our self-centeredness to die and thus find life. Lewis writes,

In the world as we now know it, the problem is how to recover this self-surrender. We are not merely imperfect creatures who must be improved; we are, as Newman said, rebels who must lay down our arms. The first answer, then, to the question why our cure should be painful, is that to render back the will which we have so long claimed for our own, is in itself, wherever and however it is done, a grievous pain. Even in Paradise I have supposed a minimal self-adherence to be overcome, though the overcoming, and the yielding, would there be rapturous. But to surrender a self-will inflamed and swollen with years of usurpation is a kind of death.[15]

It is unusual to find a study like Lewis's on the value of pain. For all his concern to explore devilry, evil and the powers of hell as part of the real background of so-called ordinary life, far more of his writings concern the unfulfilled longing that makes us feel homeless, and our desire for heaven (see chap. 12). When we read essays like "The Weight of Glory" or the chapter on heaven in *The Problem of Pain*, such writings become a powerful incentive to take the road out of the self, if we but can. Two further such attractions that urge us to forsake self-centeredness can be seen, rather unexpectedly, in Lewis's love of books, and also from the importance of friendship in his writings and life. Lewis does not endlessly dwell on the pain of the necessary dying to self, but he points to the fact that our deepest longings can take us on that road to finding our selves by losing them. The unfulfilled desire Lewis called joy, the love of books and the love called friendship are just some of these deep human longings.

The Unexpected Dimensions of Reading

Lewis was completely aware of his bookishness. His love particularly of old books inspired his literary scholarship on the literature of the sixteenth century, the medieval allegory of love and in particular the poetry of Spenser and of Milton. It is the secret of the continued readability and freshness of his literary studies many decades after they were written. How does reading and reception of other arts relate to escaping from self-centeredness? Lewis's answer shows the complete integration between his scholarship and his fiction, even his Narnian stories for children. He writes, "In love, in virtue, in the pursuit of knowledge, and in the reception of the arts" we are going "out of the self, to correct its provincialism and heal its loneliness. . . . Obviously this process can be described either as an enlargement or as a temporary annihilation of the self. But that is an old paradox; 'he that loseth his life shall save it.'"[16] His *An Experiment in Criticism* (1961), where he says this, is in effect a deceptively simple guide to reading, distilling a lifetime's scholarship and reading, both high- and lowbrow. To quote another memorable passage:

> The man who is contented to be only himself, and therefore less of a self, is in prison. My eyes are not enough for me, I will see through those of others. Reality, even seen through the eyes of many, is not enough. I will see what others have invented. Even the eyes of all humanity are not enough. I regret that the brutes cannot write books. . . . [I]n reading great literature I become a thousand men and yet remain myself. Like the night sky in the Greek poem, I see with a myriad eyes, but it is still I who see. Here, as in worship, in love, in moral action, and in knowing, I transcend myself; and am never more myself than when I do.[17]

Here Lewis speaks of a parallel between reading and love, and a couple of pages before had mentioned how in "love we escape from our self into one other." He explored this in his book *The Four Loves*, as we saw, one of the four being that of friendship, which he deeply valued throughout his life.

The Virtues of Friendship and the Health of the Self

At first sight friendship doesn't seem to relate to self-forgetfulness. Lewis was deeply aware, however, of how friendship can be poisoned and twisted, expressed in his theme of the "inner ring." When there is such an inner ring, like-minded cronies at the real control center of a group of people reinforce self-centeredness.

Lewis saw the lure of the inner ring as a perversion of what he calls "the gift of friendship." Friendship "causes perhaps half of all the happiness in the world, and no Inner Ringer can ever have it." Unlike friendship, the desire to be on the very inside of a group leads to a perpetual anxiety, even if achieved, whereas real friendship is "snug and safe" because it is free of this desire. Lewis believed that in most associations of business and profession there were inner rings as well as the official hierarchies. "You are never formally and explicitly admitted by anyone. You discover gradually, in almost indefinable ways, that it exists and that you are outside it; and then later, perhaps, that you are inside it."[18] Inner rings provide a climate in which evil becomes easier.

The theme of the inner ring is illustrated in *That Hideous Strength*, Lewis's science-fiction story that we explored in chapter six. The lure for Mark Studdock of the inner ring of Belbury, the center of the sinister N.I.C.E., dramatically illustrates its danger as he is gradually drawn into it. We see him disintegrating as a person as he more and more gives into temptation. Lewis is not afraid to picture devilry in the attempts of those at the inner core in Belbury to corrupt Studdock to their cause. Lewis also explained the concept in an essay of the same name.[19]

So much for the perversion of friendship. How does proper friendship work to free us from the "provincialism" of our isolated selves? "You modify one another's thought; out of this perpetual dog-fight a community of mind and a deep affection emerge." That is what C. S. Lewis said about his enduring friendship with Owen Barfield, the Inkling who greatly influenced his bedrock views on imagination and myth.[20]

Lewis's writings often concern friendship, and even more often are shaped by his friendships. Characteristically, his writings, from The Chronicles of Narnia to his scholarly *The Discarded Image* (on the medieval picture of the world), seek to rehabilitate values and virtues once known and lived out in what he called the Old West. Loss of these old virtues and values, he believed, put the very future of our humanity in jeopardy. Friendship was one of the central values he sought to rehabilitate. In his life, friendships played a dramatic role, shaping and coloring his years.

Lewis took a classical view of friendship that owed much to the philosopher Aristotle, which he looked at in the light of his Christian understanding, seeing it as "the school of virtue." Properly lived out, friendship could open one's eyes to previously unseen aspects of reality. In our modern times—in the new, post-Christian West and its sphere of influence—friendship can function in a restorative way, bringing us back into contact with lost reality, drawing us out of ourselves.

A shared vision. Lewis's belief in the restorative and perception-changing nature of friendship is revealed particularly well in comments he made about two friends, Hamilton Jenkin (whom he met at Oxford as an undergraduate) and his lifelong Ulster friend Arthur Greeves.

In *Surprised by Joy* Lewis reports,

> The first lifelong friend I made at Oxford was A. K. Hamilton Jenkin, since known for his books on Cornwall. He continued (what Arthur had begun) my education as a seeing, listening, smelling, receptive creature. Arthur had his preference for the Homely. But Jenkin seemed able to enjoy everything; even

ugliness. I learned from him that we should attempt a total surrender to whatever atmosphere was offering itself at the moment; in a squalid town to seek out those very places where its squalor rose to grimness and almost grandeur, on a dismal day to find the most dismal and dripping wood, on a windy day to seek the windiest ridge.

Jenkin exhibited "a serious, yet gleeful, determination to rub one's nose in the very quiddity of each thing, to rejoice in its being (so magnificently) what it was."[21]

In *That Hideous Strength* two characters become friends through a shared vision of the "quiddity" or thereness of things. Like Lewis and Jenkin, the fictional Arthur and Camilla Denniston like weather of all descriptions. Jane, who is central to the story, is surprised to discover this when she is invited on a picnic with them on a foggy autumn day. Arthur explains: "That's why Camilla and I got married. . . . We both like Weather. It's a useful taste if one lives in England."[22]

Rather like the texts of literature, a friend provides another vantage point from which to view the world. For Lewis, his different friends opened up reality in varying ways, removing some of the provincialism of his self. Owen Barfield, for instance, was very different from Arthur Greeves, who had revealed to Lewis he was not alone in the world. Though Barfield shared with Lewis a view of what was important, and asked strikingly similar questions, the conclusions he came to usually differed radically from those of his friend. Throughout the 1920s, the two had waged what Lewis called a "Great War," a long dispute over the kind of knowledge that imagination can give. As Lewis put it, it was as if Barfield spoke his language but mispronounced it! Thinking of the dogfight their friendship often was, Owen Barfield dedicated his book *Poetic Diction* to C. S. Lewis with the words, "Opposition is true friendship."

Lewis's friendship with J. R. R. Tolkien, like that with Barfield, was based on irreducible differences as well as likenesses. Initially, the two were drawn together by a love of myth, fairytale and saga, a bond that deepened when Lewis became a Christian. There were emerging differences of temperament, churchmanship and story-telling style, however, which strained yet enriched the friendship.[23]

Guests at a common feast. Furthermore, in Lewis's group of friends, the process of opening up reality was richly interactive, a constantly moving play of light. He memorably expresses this in his chapter on friendship in *The Four Loves*. In the following excerpt, "Ronald" is Tolkien and "Charles" is Charles Williams. It captures the flavor of meetings of the Inklings, as Lewis saw them.

> In each of my friends there is something that only some other friend can fully bring out. By myself I am not large enough to call the whole man into activity; I want other lights than my own to show all his facets. Now that Charles is dead, I shall never again see Ronald's reaction to a specifically Caroline joke. Far from having more of Ronald, having him "to myself" now that Charles is away, I have less of Ronald. Hence true Friendship is the least jealous of loves. Two friends delight to be joined by a third, and three by a fourth . . . each bringing out all that is best, wisest, or funniest in all the others.[24]

Ultimately, Lewis saw a group of Christian friends (as was how he saw the Inklings) as participating in a feast in which God "has spread the board and it is He who has chosen the guests."[25]

In his own pilgrimage, C. S. Lewis surrounded himself with a variety of friends.[26] In the very ordinariness of friendship, he found a vital element in his own often difficult road toward heaven. This was friendship seen as expressing in its own way the divine love, which is in the process of ridding evil forever from the universe. Jesus, in his claim to be the incarnate God, said to his disciples, "You are my friends if you do what I command" (Jn 15:14).

The Way of Goodness and the Far Country

Narnia and Middle-Earth

Near the end of his speech to the Tempters' Training College, Screwtape speaks of many roads which might finally lead a human being to heaven. Screwtape, of course, is not a reliable guide, but it could perhaps be said that many roads also lead to hell. C. S. Lewis avoided writing anything about the nature of heaven or hell merely to satisfy desire for information about the afterlife, though he clearly tried to kindle a desire for heaven in his writings. In one place he said, "There are times when I think we do not desire heaven; but more often I find myself wondering whether, in our heart of hearts, we have ever desired anything else."[1] His concern was with the roads that led toward heaven and hell in this present life, and human salvation. Though he faced up to the powerful reality of evil and badness in human life, some of his most poetic and enchanting writing is on the glimpses of heaven that we receive and that can help us to keep on the road to heaven as we seek our fulfillment in God himself, who has given us the gift of our humanity. A similar vision of the heavenly way is found in J. R. R. Tolkien. Both Lewis and Tolkien were content to evoke heaven (and hell) with vivid and masterly images that are so part of their stories that the tales cannot be properly remembered, thought about or retold without them. Lewis typically said, when writing about heaven in *The Problem of Pain* in a way that has encouraged and inspired many thousands over the years, that this was "merely an opinion of my own without the slightest authority."[2]

What Lewis came to see as a vision of heaven played an important part in his own radical change of perception as he passed from atheism and agnosticism to a belief in God and finally Christianity. In the imagery of his story *The Pilgrim's Regress*, the vision of an island he longed for helped him to get onto the "main road" of human living, in which there was the balance of heart and of mind that avoided the deathtraps of north and south—that is, arid and rigid intellectualism on one side, or insatiable and uninhibited sensualism on the other, as we saw. It was not until the end of the journey that the modern pilgrim realized the heavenly nature of his vision and that heaven was attainable in God himself.[3]

For many years in which he was an atheist, he relished nevertheless the enchantment of Balder, Fáfnir and Irish folk lore (such as the Land of Youth) before he discovered and was able to embrace their significance as pointers to heaven. He embodied the themes of his pilgrimage in the Narnian Chronicles, themes that included glimpses of the heavenly and the attendant experience he called joy.

These themes arose more or less naturally out of the stories of Narnia because they were so close to his central vision of the nature of God, Christ and reality. These were themes that might be abstract in a work of philosophy, cosmology or systematic theology, but which become concrete and tangible in Narnia. A reader who is unaware of their Christian framework may experience these momentous themes through the stories of Narnia, just as Lewis as a sixteen-year-old atheist had, as he says, his imagination "baptized" by reading George MacDonald's *Phantastes*. Under the influence of the story, he saw all common things transformed as they were "drawn into the bright shadow" of holiness as it came out of the book and rested in "the real world."[4]

Joy

The theme of what Lewis called joy threads its way through the Chronicles, as it does through many of his writings. It may well be his hallmark. Lewis saw joy as an unquenchable longing of the spirit. The longing or unsatisfied desire was a sure sign that no part of the created world, and thus no aspect of human experience, is capable of fulfilling fallen humankind. We are dominated by a homelessness and yet by a keen sense of what home means. "The sense that in this universe we are treated as strangers," he writes, "the longing to be acknowledged, to meet with some response, to bridge some chasm that yawns between us and reality, is part of our inconsolable secret."[5] Joy, in fact, is a foretaste of ultimate reality, heaven itself, or, the same thing, our world as it was meant to be, unspoiled by the fall of humankind, and one day to be remade and restored to us. "Joy," noted Lewis, "is the serious business of Heaven."[6]

In attempting to imagine heaven as the heart of our desire, Lewis suspected that joy is "the secret signature of each soul." He confessed (in words that are worth requoting), "There are times when I think we do not desire heaven; but more often I find myself wondering whether, in our heart of hearts, we have ever desired anything else. . . . While we are, this is. If we lose this, we lose all."[7]

From his conversion in 1931 Lewis's intellectual and imaginative orientation was to Christ—his work became increasingly Christ-centered. In the Chronicles the mysterious longing that pointed to joy is most often associated with the presence, or even a hint of the presence, of Aslan, the Creator Lion:

> At the name of Aslan each one of the children felt something
> jump in his inside. . . . Susan felt as if some delicious smell or

some delightful strain of music had just floated by her. And Lucy got the feeling you have when you wake up in the morning and realise that it is the beginning of the holidays or the beginning of summer.[8]

The sensation is perhaps most emphatic in *The Voyage of the Dawn Treader*, embodied in Reepicheep's quest for Aslan's Country, and is a desire that more and more grips the other voyagers. It becomes most intense as they sail over the last sea, beyond Ramandu's country, where the water is sweet. When they drink the water, they feel "almost too well and strong to bear it." They need no food—the light itself sustains them. Then a sudden, short-lived breeze from the east, from Aslan's Country, carries a smell and music on it.

> Edmund and Eustace would never talk about it afterwards. Lucy could only say, "It would break your heart." "Why," said I, "was it so sad?" "Sad!! No," said Lucy.
>
> No one in the boat doubted that they were seeing beyond the End of the World into Aslan's Country.[9]

In portraying this theme of joy, Lewis wished, to use the words of one commentator, "to awaken a desire for love and goodness."[10] In *The Magician's Nephew*, during the creation of Narnia by Aslan's song, Frank the cabby exclaims, "Glory be! . . . I'd ha' been a better man all my life if I'd known there were things like this."[11]

In *The Lion, the Witch and the Wardrobe* the girls had desired ever since they met Aslan to bury their hands in his mane. In *The Horse and His Boy*, Shasta, the lost prince, yearns to travel to Narnia. The boy experiences a desire for northern lands. In *Prince Caspian*, the longing often manifests itself as a desire for the Old Narnia, suppressed by the modernizing tyrant Miraz. In *The Last Battle*, Emeth, a virtuous Calormene whose name means "truth" in Hebrew, has since childhood desired to serve and know Tash, the false deity, and look on his face—a desire that is fulfilled when he meets Aslan.

What Lewis called joy, or an insatiable longing that calls us to be pilgrims to a distant country, is also a strong theme in Tolkien's writings. As in Lewis, joy in Tolkien points the way toward the heavenly and to hope, even when all seems lost. Both Lewis and Tolkien desired to embody that quality in their work. Though associated with Lewis's writings, joy is distinctive too in Tolkien's fiction, and deeply valued by him, as his essay "On Fairy Stories" makes clear. It is a key feature of such stories, he believes, related to the happy ending, or eucatastrophe ("good" catastrophe), part of the consolation they endow. Tolkien believes that joy in the story marks the presence of grace from the primary world. "It denies (in the face of much evidence, if you will) universal final defeat and in so far is *evangelium*, giving a fleeting glimpse of Joy, Joy beyond the walls of the world, poignant as grief." He adds, "In such stories when the sudden 'turn' comes we get a piercing glimpse of joy, and heart's desire, that for a moment passes outside the frame, rends indeed the very web of story, and lets a gleam come through."[12]

In an epilogue to the essay, Tolkien gives more consideration to the quality of joy, linking it to the Gospel narratives, which have all the qualities of an other-worldly fairy story, while at the same time being primary world history. This doubleness intensifies the quality of joy, identifying its objective source.

In Tolkien, there is not only the quality of joy linked to the sudden turn in the story, the sense of eucatastrophe, but also this joy as inconsolable longing, or sweet desire in Lewis's sense. Dominating the entire cycle of Tolkien's tales of Middle-earth is a longing to obtain the Undying Lands of the uttermost west. The longing is often symbolized by a yearning for the sea, which lay to the west of Middle-earth and over which lay Valinor, even if by a hidden road. The sundering sea separated those who longed from the object of their desire. In real life, Tolkien was constantly attracted to the sea, whether it was evident in holidays he took at places in England such as Whitby and Filey on the Yorkshire coast, in Lyme Regis or Sidmouth on the Dorset or Devon coast, or in Cornwall.

Such longing for the sea is sharply portrayed in the central figure of Galadriel, who, since the rebellion of the elves of Noldor, had been forbidden to return to the uttermost west from Middle-earth. Her longing is poignantly captured in her song in Lórien, in *The Two Towers*.[13] She laments that no ship could come and carry her over such a wide sea of separation.

Even though he is a Wood Elf, Legolas (one of the fellowship of the Ring) grows to long for the sea and the west. It is when he first saw the sea in Gondor that it awoke a longing for the Elven home in the uttermost west. In the ages before the period of *The Lord of the Rings*, Turgon of Gondolin instructs mariners to seek a way to the west in the hope that the Valar, the lords of the west, might help him. One of them, Voronwë, "is gripped by the longing of his people, and, in the purposes of providence," leads Tuor to Gondolin to warn the city of danger.

The sea dominates the story of Eärendil the great mariner (and son of Tuor). In *The Silmarillion*, Eärendil is a key figure, with associations of Christ himself, at least as a herald of his coming. After interceding on behalf of the Elves and men of Middle-earth, in distress from the evil of Morgoth, he "sailed his ship out of the mists of the world into the seas of heaven with the Silmaril upon his brow."[14] His star in the sky was a sign of the providence of Ilúvatar, providing hope. The name Earendel in the Old English poem *Christ* provided an important seed for the growth of Tolkien's invented mythology. The story of his life and voyage is one of the earliest elements in Tolkien's fiction.

"The Voyage of Eärendil" Tolkien considered as one of four key stories of *The Silmarillion*, standing independently of the history and annals of the First Age. Tolkien wrote, "His function . . . is to find a sea-passage back to the Land of the Gods, and as ambassador persuade them to take thought again for the Exiles, to pity them, and rescue them from the Enemy."[15]

Tolkien employed the idea of finding a sea passage in the earliest versions of his stories of Middle-earth, with a haunting lost road across the western sea, and the figure of Aelfwine. Aelfwine was a mariner to whom the tales of the First Age were told. He provided a narrative framework for the tales. His name means "Elf-friend." There are several versions of the Aelfwine story, but the basic idea is that an ancient British mariner seemingly by chance finds the lost road that leads to the Uttermost West and arrives at the island of Tol Eressëa (symbolic of an England that has been lost), where he hears the tales of the Elves, revealing their history and significance for humans.

The lost road is also called the "Straight Road." Even before the changing of the world, it was difficult to sail from Middle-earth to the uttermost west. After the change, when the world became a sphere and the seas bent, some Elven ships were allowed to pass beyond the world to the undying lands. They used the straight road. It was this that was sailed by the ring bearers at the end of *The Lord of the Rings* when they departed from Grey Havens.

For me, one of Tolkien's best evocations of the sea in connection with quest and longing is his poem *Imram*.[16] This concerns the voyage of St. Brendan, one of the main Celtic saints. Tolkien altered the traditional story (a voyage of seven years in search of an otherworldly Promised Land) to fit his invented mythology. The poem was intended to be part of the "The Notion Club Papers," never completed. *Immram* is Gaelic for "voyage." *Imram* mentions the Lost Road, a "shoreless mountain" (Meneltarma) marking "the foundered land" (Númenor), a mysterious island (Tol Eressëa) with a white tree (Celeborn), and a beautiful star (Eärendil) marking the old road leading beyond the world. The names in parentheses are what these places are called in *The Silmarillion*.[17]

As a medieval scholar, Tolkien would have been aware of a number of mysterious islands in the Atlantic, some recorded on early maps in the Middle Ages from confused sightings and legend. In various medieval accounts of St. Brendan's navigations in the western sea, many islands are visited where Brendan encounters magical creatures and miraculous events.[18] As well as giving a foundation for Tolkien's *Imram*, the same stories might well have inspired some features of C. S. Lewis's *The Voyage of the Dawn Treader*. Tolkien read an early version of his *Imram* poem as part of "The Notion Club Papers" to the Inklings by August 1946, knowing that many of them would be familiar with medieval tales of St. Brendan.[19]

Donald S. Johnson finds many parallels between the medieval tales of the voyage of St. Brendan and the book of Revelation in the New Testament (written during persecution against Christians in the first century). Perhaps this is the secret of the attraction of the stories to Tolkien. Johnson writes of the medieval tales, written when the church and ordinary life were under attack from Norse invaders:

> During this three-hundred year period, there was no prospect of a normal life in Ireland, especially in the religious communities. The *Navigatio* [of St Brendan] achieved its full expression in response to forces like those that impelled the Book of Revelation. Both books tell of the "decisive struggle of Christ and his followers against Satan." The voyage of Saint Brendan is a metaphoric voyage—a journey of the soul to the Promised Land.[20]

The Sea, Islands and Lost Horizons

Now that I have introduced some elements of how the sea is associated with quest and longing for the Undying Lands in Tolkien, it is possible to broaden out more into affinities and comparisons between Tolkien's and Lewis's delightful symbolism of the sea, islands and lost horizons, all of which point toward a journey to the far country associated with the way of goodness and the fulfillment of human desire—desire that points to the proper home of the human heart.

The most significant island in Tolkien's mythology is Númenor. It lay west between Middle-earth and the Undying Lands. Númenor, shaped like a star, was given as a home to humans who were friends of the Elves by the Valar (the angelic rulers of the world) at the end of the First Age of Middle-earth. The gift was given as a reward for their faithfulness and courage in the wars against Morgoth, the supreme evil power.

Númenor is Tolkien's equivalent to Atlantis. It is a state between mortal and immortal lands. The humans of Númenor were able to speak Elvish and communed with the Elves of Tol Eressëa—the island where, in early forms of Tolkien's mythology, the ancient British mariner hears the wonderful tales of the Elves. However the Númenorians were banned from actually sailing to Tol Eressëa or setting foot on the immortal lands beyond.

In C. S. Lewis's *That Hideous Strength* he borrowed from Tolkien's mythology, though he misspelled Númenor as Numinor. In that story, Merlin's magical art was a vestige of Atlantian civilization.

Important in C. S. Lewis's *The Voyage of the Dawn Treader* is World's End Island (also called Ramandu's Island), encountered by the seafarers. It is far to the east of Narnia, across the Eastern Ocean, and is close to Aslan's Country, at the beginning of the world's end. On the island the travelers find a long table covered with a crimson cloth and known as Aslan's Table, as he placed it there. The table is stocked with food each day by flocks of great white birds. As they swoop toward the island, the birds sing an unknown human language.

Lewis's positioning of World's End Island close to Aslan's Country gives it some parallels with Tolkien's Tol Eressëa in relation to the Undying Lands. Tolkien's mythology of Middle-earth, we saw, is marked by the great sea to the west, over which lies the

Undying Lands for which the Elves longed.

The Voyage of the Dawn Treader is the story of a double quest, for seven missing Lords of Narnia and for Aslan's Country far over the Eastern Ocean. Reepicheep the mouse, one of Narnia's talking animals, is particularly seeking Aslan's Country, and his quest embodies the theme of joy the we explored earlier. During the sea journey of the *Dawn Treader* across the eastern sea, various islands are encountered, each with its own kind of adventure. As in Tolkien, there is desire for the Undying Lands over the sea, but on a simpler scale.

Distant horizons inspired both writers. A horizon can be the limit of perception or experience, and far horizons in Lewis and in Tolkien symbolize the quest of the human spirit for its true fulfillment.

In Tolkien's fiction, the Undying Lands that lay beyond the western seas were originally in a flat world. Only later did his invented cosmology come to have Middle-earth on a sphere after cataclysmic change. Lewis undoubtedly owes a debt to his friend's imagination in his creation of Aslan's Country on the edge of a flat world across the Eastern Ocean. Both, as medieval scholars, knew that thinkers in the Middle Ages were clearly aware that our world is a globe. Each chose a flat world (Tolkien only initially) because of its imaginative possibilities.

Aslan's Country, in the Narnia stories, lies high up and beyond Narnia's ocean to the east. Viewed from near World's End, Aslan's Country appears to be made up of mountains of enormous height, yet forever free of snow, clothed in grass and forests as far as the eye can see. From its summit, clouds above the Eastern Ocean look like tiny sheep. The waters of Aslan's Country quench hunger and thirst. Those approaching it find a deepening and splendid brightness that confers increasing youthfulness to those long exposed to it. Its brightness is like that experienced by Elwin Ransom when in Deep Heaven, in Lewis's science-fiction trilogy. The quality of light in Deep Heaven and near Aslan's Country has close affinities with the important theme of light in Tolkien's imagination (see chap. 4).

Tolkien may be more successful, artistically, in creating a symbol of the human heart's desire located over a great ocean. But Lewis is perhaps more successful in portraying an intermediate state in his creation of the unfallen planetary world of Perelandra (Venus), which is one of the most successful images of heaven in Christian fantasy in being at once human and numinous in quality, embodying an appropriate joy and yet demonstrating its presently unattainable nature. The paradise of Perelandra is unattainable because it is home for real humans and yet unfallen. In the world of Venus Lewis gives us a powerful image of what the new creation begun in Christ's resurrection might mean. It is an oceanic world that is a human home, whereas the sea for Tolkien represents that which sunders us from our human fulfillment. For both, however, human joy and ultimate full happiness are dependent on finding and following a road out of the self, in which the self is truly discovered, as we explored in the previous chapter.

The Road Toward Heaven in C. S. Lewis and J. R. R. Tolkien

Images of heaven as the fulfillment of human desire occur in many of Lewis's writings. One, the island in his allegorical *The Pilgrim's Regress*, has already been mentioned. Wayne Martindale's *Beyond the Shadowlands: C. S. Lewis on Heaven and Hell* goes through these in great detail, including numerous images in the Narnian Chronicles.[21] Here are a couple of examples of potent images.

At the end of Narnia, Jewel the unicorn declares of Aslan's Country, "This is the land I have been looking for all my life, though I never knew it till now."[22] Jewel's comment highlights Lewis's identification of unfulfilled desire with Aslan's Country as its true object. In *The Last Battle*, his Country is realized as the new Narnia, and indeed the new England of the world from which the children have come into Narnia. Lewis had employed some of his most abiding images of heaven in describing the approach of the voyagers to the

World's End in the earlier *Voyage of the Dawn Treader*. There Eustace, Edmund and Lucy are invited to breakfast by a Lamb. On the green grass near Aslan's Country a fire has been lit and fish is roasting on it. The setting evokes a breakfast long ago by the shore of Lake Galilee, to which the newly risen Christ invited the disciples, one of the most numinous passages in the New Testament, yet in real history. In the other sense of the end of the world, Lewis describes the apocalyptic creation of the new Narnia in *The Last Battle* in terms of a heavenly country.

Heaven approaches the unimaginable, Lewis believed, even though of course we have the biblical images to take us as far as they can in their accommodation to our present limitations. Our imagination salutes heaven, however, with a hundred images, to borrow one of Lewis's phrases. As he clearly stated, he deliberately avoided concrete description claiming to be literally about the actual afterlife. He believed that parable, allegory, fiction and other forms of metaphor are the closest that we can come to speaking in a concrete way of heaven. (Arguing for the existence of heaven and hell, defending the reality of hell, rationally putting forward the case of human immortality, expounding the need for atonement and salvation, and other aspects of doctrine and the church creeds were another matter, of course.) Their aim is to encourage us in the way of goodness, driven by a love of God, as we face the powers of evil within and without. This is why he explored heaven so much through fantasy, as in *The Voyage of the Dawn Treader* and *The Last Battle*, as well as other fiction, such as *The Great Divorce* and *Perelandra*. In *The Last Battle* the children see the land of Narnia die forever and freeze over in blackness. They are filled with regret. Later, as they walk in a fresh morning light, they wonder why everything seems strangely familiar. At last they realize that this was again Narnia, but now different—larger and more vivid, more like the real thing. It is different in the way that a real thing differs from its shadow or waking life from a dream.

Is it all in Plato? The imagery of heaven, and the way of goodness rather than of badness, that Lewis uses in *The Last Battle* is explicitly derived from the Greek philosopher Plato. (He even has Professor Kirke muttering, "It's all in Plato," so that there is no doubt.)[23] There is a contrast between copy and original, or shadow and light, which also pertains to the new or real England in contrast to the Pevensies' England of wartime and just after. Lewis also uses Plato's famous image of the Cave (albeit brilliantly adapted) in one of his most memorable sequences in *The Silver Chair*, where the Green Witch tries to persuade the children and Puddleglum in the underworld that Narnia does not exist and that their very idea of the sun is derived from the hanging lamps (a stunning portrayal by Lewis of the fashionable argument that belief in God is simply a projection of our wishes and fears).

Lewis's use of these rich images involves his well-thought-out contrast between the nature of reasoning and of imagination, one concerned with truth and the other with meaning (or the real).[24] Lewis uses platonic imagery in the context of the deliberate paganism deployed in the Chronicles, in which, for instance, Aslan owes much to the old myths of dying gods and a wildness in nature—after all, he is not a tame lion, though he is safe. Behind the Chronicles, as is also true of Lewis's earlier science fiction stories, is the medieval picture of reality, particularly of the sixteenth century, which was his specific area of scholarly expertise and dominated by Plato's thought.

The use of this old imaginative model is intended to introduce an alternative way of seeing to the reader, opening up all kinds of liberating possibilities, and introducing new experiences and sensations— "getting past the watchful dragons" that are barriers to the reception of truth and of the Christ he had chosen to follow in particular.

Lewis also brings out a painful side to following the deepest longings of the human heart to find one of the many paths to heaven.

He explores how we may escape the confines of our own selves for a larger vision of reality. Those who follow a true path to heaven can be very like the traveler in John Bunyan's *The Pilgrim's Progress*, a book deeply important to Lewis. The pilgrim has to face dangers and tribulations, finding that "shortcuts" are anything but. Bunyan writes, "Some also have wished that the nearest way to their father's house were here, that they might be troubled no more with either hills or mountains to go over, but the way is the way, and there is an end."

appendix 1

War in Heaven

The Roots of C. S. Lewis's Concern with Devilry

T he exploration of devilry, the work of dark powers, in C. S. Lewis's writing was shaped by his experience—one direct, one indirect—of two modern wars. This combined a traditional understanding with a reasoned and far-reaching response to contemporary manifestations of evil. He thus sought to rehabilitate in a modern context an olden emphasis on the dangers of the world, the flesh and the devil.[1] This included a biography of Satan that had been developed by believers over the vast period of Christendom, based on sometimes tantalizing references in Scripture that had a powerful appeal to the imagination. An actual study of biblical references to Satan and the devil, direct or indirect, easily leads to a conclusion that we know a lot less about the infernal being than we thought we did. Much imaginative joining up has been done of definitive dots scattered throughout the pages of Scripture.

Lewis was not alone in his quest to understand the present in the light of the past, with its attendant authority of the divine Word, reason and indeed language itself. A somewhat similar process went on in the ruminations and fiction of his close friend and fellow Inkling J. R. R. Tolkien.

In 1937 Tolkien published *The Hobbit*, the forerunner of his *Lord of the Rings*, which had been in gestation from the end of the 1920s. Ever since Lewis had seen a draft of it he had enthused and encouraged Tolkien in the long road to publication. *The Hobbit* has as an important theme the whole issue of evil. At that stage in his thinking, and at least in his public artistic development, Tolkien chose to represent evil in the potent traditional form of a dragon, Smaug, in his lair under the Lonely Mountain. Like his friend Lewis, Tolkien was enraptured by ancient paganism and the ability of pagan insights, symbolism and magical creatures to embody meanings that he considered to be consonant with Christian teaching and core doctrine. The imaginative vitality of his dragon in *The Hobbit* owes a very great deal to Old Norse mythology—particularly Fáfnir in *The Legend of Sigurd and Gudrún*[2]—and the great early English poem, *Beowulf*. Within a few years of working on the adult sequel to *The Hobbit*, however, Tolkien found that the Ring in that story, possessed by Gollum until found by the hobbit Bilbo, had a potency for portraying evil in its most modern, global form that far exceeded the mighty dragon—an evil evidenced for instance in the apocalyptic scenes of warfare he had experienced in the First World War. The Ring, into which Sauron (effectively, a fallen angelic being) had embedded most of himself and his power, was capable of controlling and enslaving the races of Middle-earth and was, most significantly, a machine in essence, made by diabolical technology (see chap. 4). As Tolkien's *Lord of the Rings* developed and grew in the telling, Lewis was thinking and imagining on similar lines to his friend. The similarity was so much that after the second global conflict of 1939 to 1945 Lewis characterized the modern era as the Age of the Machine, an epoch as significant as the Stone Age, Iron Age and similar. He chose his inaugural lecture at Cambridge University in 1954 to proclaim this. Ironically, and with relish, he described himself as a relic of an older, dramatically different world, a surviving dinosaur in fact.[3]

The Ancient Tradition: The World, the Flesh and the Devil

It is difficult to examine the main biblical references pertaining to the devil without constructing a coherent story, one which is likely to resemble the traditional "biography" of Satan held by the church over the centuries. In this traditional life story, the devil is created at the beginning of time as an archangel of considerable standing, called Lucifer, the Morning Star. His opposite, as Lewis points out, is not God but the archangel Michael. In his pride, Satan rebels against his Creator and the values at the foundation of the universe, such as sacrificial love, and is cast down from heaven. When the first man and woman are created on earth in God's image, marking the beginning of human history, he tempts them to disobey their Maker, and evil is thus brought into our world. Since the fall of humankind we have been caught up in a cosmic battle of evil against good that has affected every aspect of our history, as part of the curse on human beings since that fall. Satan is permitted to act in the world for a limited time, his ultimate defeat having been accomplished by the heroic death of God's Son, who became a human being at a specific point in our history, a singular event marked by the old division of time into B.C. (Before Christ) and A.D. (*Anno Domini*—In the Year of Our Lord).

This biography of the devil is most famously portrayed in one of the greatest works of literature in English, John Milton's *Paradise Lost* (1667, 1674), a work that continues to inspire and influence writers and artists to this day. It was probably the most important influence on Lewis's exploration in fiction of devilry. The poem begins:

Of Man's first disobedience, and the fruit
Of that forbidden tree whose mortal taste
Brought death into the World, and all our woe,
With loss of Eden, till one greater Man
Restore us, and regain the blissful seat,
Sing, Heavenly Muse.

In his *A Preface to Paradise Lost*, C. S. Lewis paints the devil as the supreme egotist.[4] (In chapter twelve we explored Lewis's concern with self-centeredness as the root and core of wickedness.) Lewis writes there of his debt to his friend Charles Williams, who, in writing and lecturing on Milton, "partly anticipated, partly confirmed, and most of all clarified and matured, what I had long been thinking about Milton."[5] Here is a taste of Williams, where he describes Satan's pride and egocentricity.

> Satan thinks himself impaired, and what is the result? "deep malice thence conceiving and disdain." He is full of injured merit; what is the result? "high disdain." He is the full example of the self-loving spirit, and his effort throughout the poem is to lure everyone, Eve, Adam, the angels, into that same state of self-love. His description of himself in the first two books is truthful enough—that fixt mind
>
> And high disdain from sense of injured merit
>
> That with the mightiest raised me to contend . . .
>
> But it is also ironical. Certainly Satan has this sense; only this sense has landed him in hell—and in inaccuracy. Hell is always inaccurate. . . . He [Milton] thought pride, egotism, and a proper sense of one's own rights the greatest of all temptations; he was, no doubt, like most people, subject to it. And he thought it led straight to inaccuracy and malice, and finally to idiocy and hell.[6]

Lewis is at one with Williams when he comments in his introduction to Milton, "Mere Christianity commits every Christian to believing that 'the Devil is (in the long run) an ass.'"[7] On Milton's reference to Satan revealing a "sense of injured merit," quoted by Williams, Lewis remarks, "This is a well known state of mind which we can all study in domestic animals, children, film-stars, politicians, or minor poets; and perhaps nearer home."[8] He also picks up on Williams's observation, from the poem,[9] that Satan "thinks himself impaired." "In the midst of a world of light and love, of song and feast and dance, he could find nothing to think of more interesting than his own prestige."[10] Both Lewis and Williams see the devil's insanity in viewing himself as a "self-existent being" rather than one who is a "derived being, a creature."[11]

Milton drew upon a rich intellectual and imaginative tradition in creating his epic, not least early English and other medieval poetry. An example is the seventh-century English *Genesis (A)*, author unknown, which opens in praise of the Creator of all things, heaven's ruler, and swiftly moves on to the war in heaven, in which Satan is expelled to hell. In the following extract from a 1915 translation we read:

> These angelic hosts were wont to feel joy and rapture, transcendent bliss, in the presence of their Creator: their beatitude was measureless. Glorious ministers magnified their Lord, spoke his praise with zeal, lauded the Master of their being, and were excellently happy in the majesty of God. They had no knowledge of working evil or wickedness, but dwelt in innocence forever with their Lord: from the beginning they wrought in heaven nothing but righteousness and truth, until a Prince of angels through pride strayed into sin: then they would consult their own advantage no longer, but turned away from God's lovingkindness.
>
> They had vast arrogance, in that by the might of multitudes they sought to wrest from the Lord the celestial mansions, spacious and heaven-bright. Then there fell upon them, grievously, the envy, presumption, and pride of the Angel who first began to carry out the evil plot, to weave it and promote it, when he boasted by word—as he thirsted for conflict—that he wished to own the home and high throne of the heavenly kingdom to the north.

Thereupon God became angered and hostile towards the beings whom he had formerly exalted in beauty and glory: he created for the traitors a marvelous abode as penalty for their action, namely the pangs of Hell, bitter afflictions; Our Lord called forth that abysmal joyless house of punishment to wait for the outcast keepers of souls. When he knew that it was ready, he enveloped it in eternal night and equipped it with torment, filling it with fire and fearful cold, with fume and red flame: then he commanded the terrors of suffering to increase throughout that hapless place.[12]

The poem then goes on to give an account of the creation of the world, and Adam and Eve, the first humans, followed by Satan's intervention in paradise.

Unlike such medieval poems, and Milton's *Paradise Lost*, the biblical narrative in contrast begins with God creating the universe out of nothing by his Word, with his Spirit brooding over it in its unformed state. Then comes the days of creation in which the world, the habitat of humanity is formed, with humans, the first couple, being individually made by God on the sixth and final day of creating. On the seventh day God rests from his making, and the way is clear for humans, as his entrusted agents and representatives, to shape and steward the world.[13] Adam and Eve marry in mind and body, companions and suitable helpers for each other, preventing a loneliness felt if each one's only company was creatures without language, self-sacrificial love and other traits of personhood. It is not until then that a malignant creature appears and successfully tempts the new-sprung humans to disobey a specific command of God not to eat the Tree of the Knowledge of Good and Evil. It is perhaps the first "pact" with the devil.

The malignant creature, called "the serpent," is the first biblical allusion to either Satan or his manifestations. The serpent contains or embodies in some way the powers of the fallen archangel. Evil is externalized in the serpent, in the midst of a perfect Eden. (The serpent is a little like the Un-man in *Perelandra*, who retains vestiges of the scientist Weston but is possessed or controlled by the demonic power of the dark ruling power of our planet, Thulcandra.) *Satan*, from the Hebrew, essentially means "adversary." In the Old Testament book of Job "the Satan" is part of a heavenly council made up of the "sons of God," presided over by God himself. The "sons of God" are rendered as "angels" in the Greek Septuagint translation begun in the third century B.C., to make clear that there is no suggestion of polytheism in the ancient text. The angels, including the fallen angel Satan, are not God's equal but have delegated powers—which of course, like human powers, can be twisted and misused.

In the Old Testament, in fact, references to Satan or "the Satan" are sparse, but he is clearly represented as active in pursuits that are unfavorable to human beings. He prods King David into numbering his subjects (that is, pushes him into primarily relying on his material might) as recorded in 1 Chronicles 21:1. He accuses Joshua the high priest, resulting in a divine rebuke (Zech 3:1-2). Psalm 109:6 presents as a curse having Satan, "the accuser," at one's right hand. Satan famously brings unthinkable suffering to the good man Job as he ruthlessly tests Job's integrity and uprightness. Though Satan is not often mentioned explicitly, angels however are present throughout the Old Testament. Ultimately, Satan is nothing more than a bent angel—or Unangel. He is a parasite upon the good of angel existence he has been granted.

The New Testament portrait of Satan is fuller and clearer, explaining his sinister and oppressive role in human affairs. He is linked with wicked spiritual powers and authorities that go back to the beginning of things, when he sinned against God (1 Jn 3:8). These powers are, in Milton's words, the "progeny" of Satan. His subtlety is encapsulated and embodied in the ancient serpent of Genesis 3, who tempted Eve, the mother of humanity, and through her, Adam, the head or representative of the human race. He can, we are told, appear disguised as "an angel of light" (2 Cor 11:14). His temptation of Christ in the wilderness is, with the benefit of hindsight, a prototype of the Faustian pact that has haunted Western literature since tales of sixteen-century alchemists. Early stories include the German *Faustbuch* and Christopher Marlowe's play *The Tragical History of Dr. Faustus* (1604, but written earlier), which holds out the possibility of exchanging one's soul for worldly power or gain. One of the greatest modern versions of the Faust story is Mikhail Bulgakov's *The Master and Margarita*, in which the devil visits Stalinist Moscow and there is a parallel story being rewritten of Pilate's confrontation with Jesus in the first century. "What does it profit a man," remarked Jesus in the New Testament account sometime after his ordeal in the wilderness, "to gain the whole world and forfeit his soul?" (Mk 8:36). Possibly the earlier temptation of Adam and Eve alludes to a similar type of pact— ironically, an exchange of knowledge of good and evil for death.

The wider New Testament context of evil amidst spiritual powers and authorities connects with the Old Testament hint of Satan as part of the angelic governance of the cosmos, in which he is allowed temporary powers. Devilry in the universe, though focused on this powerful adversary of human beings, encompasses all kinds of manifestations of the demonic, changing with cultural and historical developments. In the Old Testament period pagan gods like Beelzebub, the "lord of the flies," were seen as idols, demonic in their control over their worshipers, leading to inhumanity (such as child sacrifice, violation of women and sexual perversion—male and female prostitution in the temples). The idols and demonic manifestations of our time are not likely to take the same shape as those in the first century, when Christ was active on earth, and in the early generations of the church. Yet, according to historic Christian doctrine, a consistent malevolence lies behind all such manifestations, shaped by a cold and ruthless intelligence inimical to human welfare and absorbed in its self-gratification and rebellion against God. The New Testament records Satan's persistent activity in human affairs, as well as revealing his inevitable destruction—a fate determined by his effective defeat at Christ's death on the cross, which was, in Augustine's vivid phrase, "the devil's mousetrap."

> The devil was conquered by his own trophy of victory. The devil jumped for joy, when he seduced the first man and cast him down to death. By seducing the first man, he slew him; by slaying the last man, he lost the first from his snare. The victory of our Lord Jesus Christ came when he rose, and ascended into heaven; then was fulfilled what you have heard when the Apocalypse was being read, "The Lion of the tribe of Judah has won the day" [Rev 5:5]. . . . The devil jumped for joy when Christ died; and by the very death of Christ the devil was overcome: he took, as it were, the bait in the mousetrap. He rejoiced at the death, thinking himself death's commander. But that which caused his joy dangled the bait before him. The Lord's cross was the devil's mousetrap: the bait which caught him was the death of the Lord.[14]

The biblical picture of Satan and his manifestations is presented both in didactic statements (such as "prince of the power of the air," "adversary" and "accuser") and in vivid images that have attracted the imaginations of writers and artists over the ages—including war in heaven, Satan falling like lightning in his defeat, a dragon, the subtle serpent in Eden, and hell's lake of fire and brimstone created for him. Though Lewis in *The Screwtape Letters* and *That Hideous Strength* employed modern images in his portrayal of devilry as bureaucracy or the rule of the few over the many by quasi-scientific methods, one of his most fundamental images comes from the biblical portrait. This is his location of hell as downward or "low," as when Screwtape speaks of his infernal master as "Our Father Below" or refers to the Lowerarchy of hell. This is in contrast to the properly spiritual, the good and God himself as higher or high. This imagery of high and low is surprisingly persistent in English and perhaps other languages.

We speak, for instance, of high culture, high art, highways, the higher life, higher animals and the higher processes of the brain. Even degrees and higher degrees conferred by universities imply steps upward. The Bible itself is replete with references to high priests as well as to "high places," which, though usually higher in altitude than surrounding land, have greater significance than their measurable height. The image of height is thus an essential element in articulating our response of worship, admiration or reverence, whether to the Most High God or to qualities of the created world and people that we greatly value.

Thus when Satan is consigned to a "bottomless pit" in Revelation 20:1, this is the most extreme antithesis possible to the glory of height and its epitome in God's exalted throne. The debasement and lowness of Satan ties in with other traditional or stock images of evil, such as darkness as opposed to light, a traditional repertoire that Lewis was constantly trying to rehabilitate for modern readers. He, like Tolkien and other modern writers, however, also employed new images in response to contemporary manifestations of evil. The supreme image was that of the machine, or techniques in human attitudes and behaviors that had become mechanical, where the human is automaton rather than autonomous. In this Lewis, like Tolkien, had affinities with cultural analysts as Marshall McLuhan, Jacques Ellul and Martin Heidegger.[15]

It is not only the machine but the machine coming to carry—to externalize or objectify—supernatural qualities of demonic perversion. Rather as a charm is endued with human hopes and attempted influence over luck, the machine then, in the view of Lewis and Tolkien, as well as others, is embodied with malice toward humanity. Nature as seen in the past is replaced today by an intelligent artificial Other, a machine that is allowed to ride over the human. For Lewis this is an inevitable result of espousing a materialist view of life in combination with wizard-like technological powers. To paraphrase Marshall McLuhan, technologies are extensions of man. It follows that if humans see themselves only as biological machines that replicate, their technological extensions of their bodily powers are vacant, ready for demonic possession. Any human qualities are overridden. Lewis's Un-man leads to the antihuman Age of the Machine in Lewis's nightmare vision. Heidegger, optimistic like Dr. Frankenstein that technology will be mastered, wrote that "The will to mastery becomes all the more urgent the more technology threatens to slip from human control."[16] In one of his letters to Wormwood, Screwtape speculates,

> I have great hopes that we shall learn in due time how to emotionalize and mythologize their science to such an extent that what is, in effect, a belief in us (though not under that name) will creep in while the human mind remains closed to belief in the Enemy. . . . If once we can produce our perfect work—the Materialist Magician, the man, not using, but veritably worshipping, what he vaguely calls "Forces" while denying the existence of "spirits"—then the end of the war will be in sight.[17]

appendix 2

The Spirit of the Age

Subjectivism

We see a C. S. Lewis who, as a contemporary writer, is thoroughly steeped in a biblical and traditional view of evil and devilry. He drew upon both the imaginative and intellectual roots of this view. He saw characteristically modern manifestations of devilry as being allowed to come about through a far-reaching modern malady he called "subjectivism."[1] He presented the cause (subjectivism) and the result (a power that has become diabolical in intent and even in practice) in an essay and a small philosophical book, both written in 1943, the year of the Warsaw Uprising, the RAF Dambusters raid and the start of round-the-clock bombing of German cities by the Allies. The essay was "The Poison of Subjectivism," which appeared in the journal *Religion and Life* (vol. 12) in the summer, and the book was *The Abolition of Man*, published in January of that year by Oxford University Press. He had also touched on the themes imaginatively that same year in *Perelandra* (1943), and earlier in *Out of the Silent Planet* (1938) and *The Screwtape Letters* (1942). He focused more strongly however on the theme of subjectivism and devilry in the last volume of the science-fiction trilogy, *That Hideous Strength* (1945).

What then does Lewis mean by "subjectivism"? He explains in "The Poison of Subjectivism":

> Until modern times no thinker of the first rank ever doubted that our judgments of value were rational judgments or that what they discovered was objective. It was taken for granted that in temptation passion was opposed, not to some sentiment, but to reason. Thus Plato thought, thus Aristotle, thus Hooker, Butler and Doctor Johnson. The modern view is very different. It does not believe that value judgments are really judgments at all. They are sentiments, or complexes, or attitudes, produced in a community by the pressure of its environment and its traditions, and differing from one community to another. To say that a thing is good is merely to express our feeling about it; and our feeling about it is the feeling we have been socially conditioned to have.[2]

Nearly seventy years after this article was published, this kind of subjectivism has recognizably deepened, despite the lessons of World War II. Values that were once seen as objective, absolute or universal are sometimes today even perceived as tools used by interest groups to exert power and authority over others. Lewis argued the reverse of this. Rather than qualities like goodness, love and similar values being power structures—even tools of oppression—they are in reality common to humanity and definitive to what makes us human. They indeed limit, check and subvert the self-interested and self-absorbed powers that seek to subjugate human beings. Looking at his own time Lewis believed that the Nazis with their "Thousand Year" Reich exerted their malign power because of their subjectivism—they were not self-regulated by objective principles such as justice and the view that racism and anti-Semitism are terribly wrong. Lewis remarked in the 1943 article,

Everyone is indignant when he hears the Germans define justice as that which is to the interest of the Third Reich. But it is not always remembered that this indignation is perfectly groundless if we ourselves regard morality as a subjective sentiment to be altered at will. Unless there is some objective standard of good, overarching Germans, Japanese, and ourselves alike whether any of us obey it or no, then of course the Germans are as competent to create their ideology as we are to create ours. If "good" and "better" are terms deriving their sole meaning from the ideology of each people, then of course ideologies themselves cannot be better or worse than one another.[3]

In his small philosophical book *The Abolition of Man*, concerned with modern education of children, Lewis developed his argument against the "poison" of subjectivism. In a letter in 1955 he ruefully commented that *The Abolition of Man* "is almost my favourite among my books but in general has been almost totally ignored by the public."[4]

This powerful tract defends the objectivity of values like goodness and beauty over against the modern view that the mind of the beholder projects human emotions and subjective states onto external things, and that the mind that does this projection is simply reflecting the social attitudes of a culture. In contrast, Lewis argues that "Until quite modern times all teachers and even all men believed the universe to be such that certain emotional reactions on our part could be either congruous or incongruous to it—believed, in fact, that objects did not merely receive, but could *merit*, our approval or disapproval, our reverence or our contempt."[5]

If values are objective, argued Lewis, one person may be right and another wrong in describing qualities in things. Think of the most beautiful waterfall you know. Two people may be looking at a such a waterfall. If one says that a waterfall is beautiful and another says that it is not, that *beautiful* does not merely describe emotions within the beholder. Lewis goes deeper than this, however. Clyde S. Kilby explains,

> Lewis is concerned with the problem of objective values, whether for instance saying that a waterfall is "sublime" means only that one has the emotion of sublimity while looking at it. If a waterfall is sublime to one person and contemptible to another, does that mean that all values are thereby subjective and even trivial? Or is there a "given," a quality put into things from the outside which demands a certain response whether we happen to make that response or not?[6]

Only one of the beholders is right; their opinions are not equally valid. A similar situation exists over the goodness or badness of an action. Judging goodness or badness is not simply a matter of opinion. Lewis argued indeed that there is a universal acknowledgment of good and bad over matters like theft, murder, rape and adultery, a sense of what Lewis called the Tao. "The human mind has no more power of inventing a new value than of imagining a new primary colour, or, indeed, of creating a new sun and a new sky for it to move in."[7] What Lewis is getting at may be partly understood in terms of competence, I think. Appreciation of goodness and awareness of badness may only be cultivated in the sense of someone mastering a musical instrument or learning to read. In both cases there is adjustment: in the one to what is a good performance and in the other to what constitutes competent reading. In either example there are norms that are objective and have to be recognized—we conform to them and, in a sense, surrender ourselves to them.

Abandonment of the Tao, or the Way, as is so much a characteristic of modern thought for Lewis, spells total disaster, he believed, for the human race. Specifically human values like freedom and dignity become meaningless, Lewis felt; the human being is merely part of nature (that is, nature seen materialistically). Nature, including humanity, is to be conquered by the technical appliance of science. Technology, with no limits or moral checks on it, becomes totalitarian—it is now technocracy. As technocracy advances, the control of the human race falls into fewer and fewer hands. An elite plans the future generations, and the present generation is cut off from the past. Such an elite is conceivably the most demonic example of what Lewis called the "inner ring." It is a social and cultural embodiment of what, in an individual, would be deemed self-absorption and egoism.

Lewis elsewhere sums up his point:

> At the outset the universe appears packed with will, intelligence, life and positive qualities; every tree is a nymph and every planet a god. Man himself is akin to the gods. The advance of knowledge gradually empties this rich and genial universe: first of its gods, then of its colours, smells, sounds and tastes, finally of solidity itself as solidity was originally imagined. As these items are taken from the world, they are transferred to the subjective side of the account: classified as our sensations, thoughts, images or emotions. The Subject becomes gorged, inflated, at the expense of the object. But the matter does not end there. The same method which has emptied the world now proceeds to empty ourselves. The masters of the method soon announce that we were just as mistaken (and mistaken in much the same way) when we attributed "souls," or "selves" or "minds" to human organisms, as when we attributed Dryads to the trees. . . . We, who have personified all other things, turn out to be ourselves personifications. . . . And thus we arrive at a result uncommonly like zero.[8]

The Abolition of Man is essentially a contemporary defense of natural law—the idea of qualities like goodness, justice, wrong and similar attributes being real characteristics of nature, not our projections onto things. Lewis attempts to rehabilitate the approach to virtue of the premodernist "Old West," the common presupposition of the Greco-Roman and Judeo-Christian traditions. In fact, he argued in the book that the virtues are universal, not merely old Western. An objective morality is an essential property of our very humanity.

The book points to a central feature of Lewis's understanding of what has gone wrong in the modern world. He never extends this analysis in a whole book,[9] but it is implicit to or touched on in a number of his analytical and fictional works. This modern error is the convergence of a utilitarian (rather than proper) science and the magical—and even the demonic.

> There is something which unites magic and applied science while separating both from the wisdom of earlier ages. For the wise men of old the cardinal problem had been how to conform the soul to reality, and the solution had been knowledge, self-discipline, and virtue. For magic and applied science alike the problem is how to subdue reality to the wishes of men: the solution is a technique; and both, in the practice of this technique, are ready to do things hitherto regarded as disgusting and impious—such as digging up and mutilating the dead.
>
> If we compare the chief trumpeter of the new era (Bacon) with Marlowe's Faustus, the similarity is striking. You will read in some critics that Faustus has a thirst for knowledge. In reality, he hardly mentions it. It is not truth he wants from the devils, but gold and guns and girls. . . . In the same spirit Bacon condemns those who value knowledge as an end in itself: this, for him, is to use as a mistress for pleasure what ought to be a spouse for fruit. The true object is to extend Man's power to the performance of all things possible. He rejects magic because it does not work; but his goal is that of the magician. In Paracelsus the characters of magician and scientist are combined. . . . It might be going too far to say that the modern

scientific movement was tainted from its birth: but I think it would be true to say that it was born in an unhealthy neighbourhood and at an inauspicious hour. Its triumphs may have been too rapid and purchased at too high a price: reconsideration, and something like repentance, may be required.[10]

The convergence of scientism (the misuse of proper science) and subjectivism highlights, for Lewis, an unprecedented threat to the future of human beings. Even as an image, it can indicate powerfully, for example, in its manifestation in modern wars, devilry at work behind the scenes in a supernatural world. A blind faith in progress, and its attendant chronological snobbery, is out of touch with reality, Lewis clearly thought. Tolkien had a similar view. Having lived through two global wars, Lewis tried to write appropriately in the light of a cosmic struggle that was reflected in those world wars. He didn't need or even want to say, I think, that any further world war, if future generations are to be cursed with it, is likely to escalate the destruction of human life on a massive scale hinted at in previous conflicts. His concern was rather the destruction of human beings in their very humanity, and to write of hope and salvation in a way that was still convincing when bombs were exploding or when bereavement and pain were experienced. Tolkien, for his part, denied that the Ring in *The Lord of the Rings* was an allegory of the atomic bomb. What it symbolized, in fact, was something far worse—power that becomes demonic by misused technology, slavery and other forms of oppression. The actions of the humble hobbits Frodo and Sam in helping to destroy the Ring represented, in fact, weakness overcoming the strong and powerful by a providential action motivated by love for what included those Screwtape called the "human vermin."

Acknowledgments

This book has been many years in writing, and hence has built up a number of debts to those upon whom I tried out various ideas, directly and indirectly. Talks turned into published book chapters or magazine articles. These all played their part in the content of this book. One primary seed was a talk I gave at an inspired conference in North Wales in 2006 on demonology, which explored "the lure of the dark side" in contemporary culture, including film and music as well as literature. My talk featured two modern figures of perversion, Voldemort from the Harry Potter stories, with his sinister horcruxes, and Sauron the Dark Lord from *The Lord of the Rings*, with his Ring of Power. This led me to think more widely about modern manifestations and depictions of good and evil, my mind turning to the portrayal of hell and the devices it used in a modern war setting in C. S. Lewis's *The Screwtape Letters*.

Thanks, then, to Professor Christopher Partridge for inviting me to speak on devilry at his conference. Thanks, also, to *Silver Leaves* (issue 2, 2008), and its special issue on the Inklings, which allowed me to explore devilry and images of evil in Tolkien. I earlier used similar material in a talk to the Tolkien Society. The Bible Society commissioned an article on C. S. Lewis and heaven ("The Far Country: C. S. Lewis's Vision of Heaven in the Chronicles of Narnia,"

The Bible in Transmission, winter 2008), which I have drawn upon, with their permission. Bruce L. Edwards kindly agreed to my adapting some of a chapter I wrote on Lewis's experiences during World War I for his four-volume *C. S. Lewis: Life, Works, and Legacy* (Praeger Perspectives, 2007). My exploration of the theme of light in Tolkien is partly adapted from my book *Tolkien and The Lord of the Rings: A Guide to Middle-earth* (Mahwah, NJ: Paulist Press, 2001), as is my account of his short story, "Leaf by Niggle," with the publisher's permission. My look at Lewis's *Till We Have Faces, The Cosmic Trilogy* and *The Four Loves* partly draws upon *The C. S. Lewis Encyclopedia* (Wheaton, IL: Crossway, 2000).

It remains to thank my editors Cindy Bunch and Drew Blankman, and art director Cindy Kiple, in particular, from the ever helpful staff of InterVarsity Press in Illinois, as well as others who gave me feedback on the book in preparation.

Notes

Introduction

[1] Richard Matheson, *What Dreams May Come* (New York: Tor Books, 2004), p. 7 (italics removed).

[2] C. S. Lewis, *The Great Divorce* (New York: Macmillan, 1946), pp. 7-8.

[3] C. S. Lewis, *The Problem of Pain* (London: Geoffrey Bles, 1940), chap. 8.

[4] C. S. Lewis, "Weight of Glory," in *The Weight of Glory and Other Addresses* (1941; repr., Grand Rapids: Eerdmans, 1965), p. 5.

[5] The link between Sayers and Williams is established in Lewis's preface to a collection of essays in memory of Williams: *Essays Presented to Charles Williams*, ed. C. S. Lewis (Grand Rapids: Eerdmans, 1966).

Chapter 1: C. S. Lewis in Wartime

[1] *London Times*, July 20, 1940, p. 4, quoted in *The Collected Letters of C. S. Lewis*, ed. Walter Hooper, vol. 2, *Books, Broadcasts and War 1931–1949*, (London: HarperCollins, 2004), p. 425.

[2] C. S. Lewis, letter to W. H. Lewis, dated by him July 20, 1940, in Hooper, *Collected Letters*, 2:425.

[3] The phrase "the world, the flesh and the devil" comes from the version of the Book of Common Prayer used at that time by Anglican (Episcopal) churches in the Service of Baptism. See a possible biblical source in Ephesians 2:1-3.

[4] Lewis reveals this for instance in a letter to Arthur Greeves when later he was studying in Bookham, in which he says that he has spoken to nobody but his tutor and Mrs. Kirkpatrick all the week. He added, "not of course that I mind, much less complain; on the contrary, I find that the people whose society I prefer to my own are very few and far between." Letter to Arthur Greeves, November 17, 1914, in *Collected Letters of C. S. Lewis*, ed. Walter Hooper, vol. 1, *Family Letters 1905–1931* (London: HarperCollins, 2004), p. 94.

[5] John Garth, *Tolkien and the Great War: The Threshold of Middle-Earth* (New York: Mariner, 2005), p. 8.

[6]Ibid., p. 9.

[7]West Midlands corresponds to an ancient region of central England, now including the modern counties of Staffordshire, Warwickshire, Worcestershire, Herefordshire and Shropshire, and the metropolitan regions of Birmingham and Wolverhampton. Tolkien famously based the Shire of Middle-earth on this, his home area.

[8]The village of Bookham encompasses Great and Little Bookham. The cottage at which Lewis stayed, the home of Mr. and Mrs. Kirkpatrick in Great Bookham, no longer exists. Lewis in his letters from this period refers to where he was staying both as Bookham and as Great Bookham. For more on Bookham, see www.bookhamvillage.co.uk.

[9]See Lewis's letter to Albert Lewis from Bookham, October 22, 1915, in Hooper, *Collected Letters*, 1:147. There were a number of zeppelin attacks aimed at London at this time, with a number of civilian casualties.

[10]In the United Kingdom, the academic year is divided into three terms, the autumn (fall) term, the spring term and the summer term. The Easter vacation divides the spring and summer terms. The Oxford terms Michaelmas, Hilary and Trinity correspond to the autumn, spring and summer terms.

[11]Oral History interview with Maureen Moore, the Marion E. Wade Archive, Wheaton College, Wheaton, IL.

[12]Lewis, letter to Albert Lewis, June 10, 1917, in Hooper, *Collected Letters*, 1:317.

[13]K. J. Gilchrist, *A Morning After War: C. S. Lewis and World War I* (New York: Peter Lang, 2005), p. 125.

[14]Hooper, *Collected Letters*, 1:341. Lewis warmly reminisces about Johnson in C. S. Lewis, *Surprised by Joy* (London: Geoffrey Bles, 1955), chap. 12.

[15]Ibid., p. 342.

[16]See Lewis's poem "French Nocturne," in *Spirits in Bondage*, www.gutenberg.org/files/2003/2003-h/2003-h.htm#link2H_PART1.

[17]Gilchrist, *Morning After War*, p. 76.

[18]Second Lieutenant E. F. C. Moore's death would not be confirmed officially until September.

[19]*The Lewis Papers: Memoirs of the Lewis Family: 1850-1930*, ed. W. H. Lewis (unpublished, Wade Center Archives, Wheaton College), 5:308.

[20]R. L. Green and W. Hooper, *C. S. Lewis: A Biography*, rev. and exp. ed. (London: HarperCollins, 2002), p. 44.

[21]For an analysis of his thought and its development at this period, see David C. Downing, *The Most Reluctant Convert: C. S. Lewis's Journey to Faith* (Downers Grove, IL: InterVarsity Press, 2002).

[22]For a thorough study into the variety of and similarities in mystical experience see Christopher Partridge and Theodore Gabriel, eds., *Mysticisms East and West: Studies in Mystical Experience* (Carlisle, UK: Paternoster, 2003).

[23]C. S. Lewis, "Satan Speaks," Project Gutenberg, www.gutenberg.org /files/2003/2003-h/2003-h.htm.

[24]Lewis, *Lewis Papers*, 6:79.

[25]C. S. Lewis, "Learning in War-Time," a sermon preached in the Church of St. Mary the Virgin, Oxford, Autumn 1939.

[26]This appears to be the opposite of what is argued in Gilchrist's *A Morning After War*, that Lewis suppressed the reality of his wartime experience because it devastated his romantic beliefs that integrated his life. In *Dymer* (1926, his narrative poem) he was able to face the end of romantic ideals. Gilchrist is completely right, however, I think, in concluding, "The things Lewis met in France and the fragments—metal or metaphorical—that he carried within him from that place gave him a knowledge of grief, of loss, of the atrocities that humankind is capable of producing, of relationships awry and relationships lost, of the wanderings of youth—knowledge that after his conversion continued to inform his views of life, the cosmos, and his faith beyond a point where many people can follow" (p. 218).

[27]For more see my *The Oxford Inklings: Lewis, Tolkien and Their Circle* (Oxford: Lion, 2015).

[28]T. S. Eliot, introduction to Charles Williams, *All Hallows Eve* (New York: Farrar, Straus & Giroux, 1977), p. xiv.

[29]C. S. Lewis, *Of This and Other Worlds*, ed. Walter Hooper (London: Collins, 1982), p. 79.

[30]Screwtape's academic prowess particularly can be seen in his after-dinner speech to the Tempter's Training College, to be found in the short story "Screwtape Proposes a Toast," included in recent editions of *The Screwtape Letters* but written many years after the *Letters*. As in *The Screwtape Letters*, the "voice" of Screwtape in the speech is often reminiscent of Lewis's (without hell's twisted perspective, of course). Screwtape speaks of political and social changes, and their implications for education, with ease.

[31]J. R. R. Tolkien, letter to Christopher Tolkien, in *Letters of J. R. R. Tolkien*,

ed. Humphrey Carpenter (London: George Allen & Unwin, 1981), letter 96, p. 111.

[32]Ibid., letter 66, p. 78.

Chapter 2: Devilry and the Problem of Hell

[1]C. S. Lewis, preface to "Screwtape Proposes a Toast," in *The Screwtape Letters*, rev. ed. (New York: Macmillan, 1961), p. 151.

[2]C. S. Lewis, *Miracles*, rev. ed. (New York: CollinsFontana, 1960), p. 125.

[3]Gareth Knight, *The Magical World of the Inklings* (Shaftsbury, UK: Element Books, 1990), pp. 236-37. See Owen Barfield, *Orpheus: A Poetic Drama* (West Stockbridge, MA: Lindisfarne Press, 1983).

[4]See John Buchan, *The Thirty-Nine Steps*, chap. 8, Project Gutenberg, www.gutenberg.org/files/558/558-h/558-h.htm.

[5]As I write this, the *London Times* today has a large, front-page headline: "Hawking: God Did Not Create Universe," the story of which includes the sentence "Just as Darwinism removed the need for a creator in the sphere of biology, Britain's most eminent scientist argues that a new series of theories have rendered redundant the role of a creator for the Universe" (September 2, 2010). The same distinguished mathematician and physicist almost in the same breath can speak of the rational likelihood of alien beings existing and the dangers of being in contact with them ("Stephen Hawking Warns Over Making Contact with Aliens," *BBC News*, April 25, 2010, http://news.bbc.co.uk/2/hi/8642558.stm). It is perfectly plausible in a secular climate to believe in alien beings in outer space but not supernatural beings.

[6]Friedrich Nietzsche, *The Gay Science*, trans. Walter Kaufmann (New York: Vintage, 1974), 3.132.

[7]Preface to *The Screwtape Letters and Screwtape Proposes a Toast* (London: Geoffrey Bles, 1966), p. 11.

[8]C. S. Lewis, *That Hideous Strength* (London: Bodley Head, 1945), pp. 298-99.

[9]C. E. M. Joad, review of *The Screwtape Letters*, by C. S. Lewis, *New Statesman and Nation*, May 16, 1942.

[10]C. S. Lewis, *The Abolition of Man* (London: Oxford University Press, 1943).

[11]C. S. Lewis, preface to "Screwtape Proposes a Toast," in *The Screwtape Letters: With Screwtape Proposes a Toast* (New York: Macmillan, 1982), p. 151.

[12]Ibid., p. 169.

[13]Ibid., p. 168.

[14]Ibid., p. 170.

[15]Lewis was also, of course, constantly exposed to the conversations of his two American stepsons, David and Douglas Gresham.

[16]John Macgowan (1726–1780). Baptist minister and popular author—see Charlotte Fell-Smith, "Macgowan, John (1726–1780)," rev. J. H. Y. Briggs, *Oxford Dictionary of National Biography* (Oxford: Oxford University Press, 2004), accessed July 28, 2014, www.oxforddnb.com/view/article/17516.

[17]Lewis mentions hearing about a book that in some interesting respects fits the description of Macgowan's satire, though Macgowan's is eighteenth century not seventeenth, and records diabolical conversations rather than being letters from a demon. Macgowan's however is concerned with contemporary social and political comment. Lewis writes, "I am told that I was not first in the field and that someone in the seventeenth century wrote letters from a devil. I have not seen that book. I believe its slant was mainly political" (preface to *Screwtape Letters*, p. 11). A nineteenth-century book titled *Letters From Hell* was read by Lewis and was published in several editions, including one with a preface by George MacDonald—its author was the Dane Valdemar Adolph Thisted. Its structure however is quite dissimilar to *The Screwtape Letters*, though self-centeredness is a central theme it shares with *The Screwtape Letters*.

[18]John Macgowan, *Infernal Conference; or Dialogues of Devils* (London: Milner, n.d), p. 7.

[19]A. N. Wilson, *C. S. Lewis: A Biography* (New York: W. W. Norton, 1990), p. 93.

[20]Lewis's insight into the importance of details of ordinary life (and their place in leading us to heaven or hell) may also be seen in his 1948 brief essay "The Trouble with 'X' . . ." in *God in the Dock: Essays on Theology*, ed. Walter Hooper (London: Collins Fount, 1979), pp. 74-78.

Chapter 3: Inklings in Wartime

[1]Documentation of the Inklings is very patchy. It was not an instituted society with formal membership and minute taking. For a knowledge of meetings, we have to rely on comments mainly in letters, diaries, biographies or studies by those who personally knew or met members (e.g., George Sayer, Roger Lancelyn Green, Chad Walsh), or recorded reminiscences (often made very many years later).

[2]There is a copy of "Angels at Bay" in the Wade Center, Wheaton College,

Wheaton, Illinois.

[3]J. R. R. Tolkien, letter to Christopher Tolkien, June 3, 1945, in *Letters of J. R. R. Tolkien*, ed Humphrey Carpenter (London: George Allen & Unwin, 1981), p. 116.

[4]Winston Churchill, quoted in Stephen Bungay, "His Speeches: How Churchill Did It," *The Churchill Centre*, accessed October 31, 2014, www.winstonchurchill.org/learn/speeches/speeches-about-winston-churchill/his-speeches-how-churchill-did-it.

[5]John D. Mabbott, *Oxford Memories* (Oxford: Thorntons, 1986), p. 91.

[6]C. S. Lewis, letter to W. H. Lewis, November 11, 1939, in *C. S. Lewis: Collected Letters*, ed. Walter Hooper, vol. 2, *Books, Broadcasts and War 1931–1949* (London: HarperCollins, 2004), pp. 288-89.

[7]See J. R. R. Tolkien, *The Return of the Shadow*, ed. Christopher Tolkien (London: Unwin Hyman, 1988), pp. 369-411.

[8]This phrase is used in a quotation placed by Lewis in his *That Hideous Strength*: "the Shadow of that hyddeous strength/Sax myle and more it is of length" (Sir David Lindsay, c. 1490–1555). Lewis takes the lines from a description of the Tower of Babel.

[9]Charles Williams, *The House by the Stable*, in Charles Williams, *Seed of Adam and Other Plays*, ed. Anne Ridler (London: Oxford University Press, 1948), pp. 45-46.

[10]See Rand Kuhl, "Owen Barfield in Southern California," *Mythlore* 1, no. 4 (1969).

[11]C. S. Lewis, ed., *Essays Presented to Charles Williams* (London: Oxford University Press, 1947), p. xiii.

[12]C. S. Lewis, "Myth Became Fact," in *Essay Collection and Other Short Pieces* (London: Harper Collins, 2000), p. 140.

[13]See the entry "Death" in Colin Duriez, *Tolkien and The Lord of the Rings: a Guide to Middle-earth* (Mahwah, NJ: HiddenSpring, 2001), pp. 162-64.

[14]Draft letter to Peter Hastings, September 1954, in *Letters of J. R. R. Tolkien*, ed. Humphrey Carpenter (London: George Allen & Unwin, 1981), letter 153.

[15]Sebastian D. G. Knowles, *A Purgatorial Flame: Seven British Writers in the Second World War* (Philadelphia: University of Pennsylvania Press, 1990), p. 17.

[16]John Wain, "Oxford," in *Sprightly Running* (London: St. Martin's Press, 1962), p. 149.

[17]"Introductory," in C. S. Lewis, *Arthurian Torso: Containing the Post-*

humous Fragment of the Figure of Arthur by Charles Williams and A Commentary on the Arthurian Poems of Charles Williams (London: Oxford University Press, 1948).

[18]Wain, *Sprightly Running*, p. 184.

[19]Robert E. Havard, "Philia: Jack at Ease," in *C. S. Lewis at the Breakfast Table and Other Reminiscences*, ed. James T. Como (London: Collins, 1980), p. 217.

[20]Although affirming that the Inklings were made up of Christians, Lewis's brother Warren made it clear the informal club of friends had no explicit agenda, such as being a literary movement. Its character and concerns arose from its individual members. For a full exploration of the nature of the group, see my *The Oxford Inklings: Lewis, Tolkien and Their Circle* (Oxford: Lion, 2015).

[21]W. H. Lewis, in *Brothers and Friends: The Diaries of Major Warren Hamilton Lewis*, ed. Clyde S. Kilby and Marjorie Lamp Mead (San Francisco: Harper & Row, 1982), pp. 184-85.

Chapter 4: Images of the Dark Side

[1]The subjective view of evil is not to be confused with subjectiv*ism* as a malady of modern thought, which is discussed in appendix 1. See Tom Shippey, *The Road to Middle-earth*, rev. and exp. ed. (New York: Houghton Mifflin, 2003), pp. 140-50.

[2]Augustine's early thought was shaped by Plato, but he eventually became distinctly Christian as he struggled with the nonrational nature of the human will and the central role it played in the origins of evil in the world. Platonic thought in its various manifestations lacks Augustine's radical view of evil and sin, which sees evil as having no substance, and God's created universe, and thus existence itself, as being good. See "Saint Augustine," *Stanford Encyclopedia of Philosophy*, updated November 12, 2010, http://plato.stanford.edu/entries/augustine.

[3]Tom Shippey, *The Road to Middle-earth: How J. R. R. Tolkien Created a New Mythology* (London: Allen & Unwin, 1982), p. 108.

[4]See Ralph Wood's rejection of the charge of Manichaeanism in his "Tolkien's Augustinian Understanding of Good and Evil: Why *The Lord of the Rings* Is Not Manichean," in *Tree of Tales: Tolkien, Literature and Theology*, ed. Trevor Hart and Ivan Khovacs (Waco, TX: Baylor University Press, 2007), pp. 85-102.

[5]It may be that as a result of choices as well as biological engineering Orcs

became implacably evil but originally possessed at least some goodness. Like demons, who were originally angels, they may be fallen creatures who have gone beyond salvation. The nomenclature of Lewis's demons (Screwtape, Wormwood, Slubgob, etc.) have some similarity to the names of Orcs Sam and Frodo encounter in Mordor.

[6]George MacDonald, *A Dish of Orts* (London: Sampson Low, 1893), p. 316. Lewis underlined this quote from MacDonald in his personal copy of *A Dish of Orts*, which is now held at the Wade Center, Wheaton College.

[7]Colin Duriez and David Porter, *The Inklings Handbook* (St. Louis: Chalice Press, 2001), pp. 102-3.

[8]Augustine, *Confessions*, bk. 7, trans. Edward Bouverie Pusey, Project Gutenberg, updated May 16, 2013, www.gutenberg.org/files/3296/3296-h /3296-h.htm#link2H_4_0007.

[9]C. S. Lewis, *English Literature in the Sixteenth Century Excluding Drama* (Oxford: Clarendon Press, 1954), pp. 3-4.

[10]C. S. Lewis, "De Descriptione Temporum," in *Selected Literary Essays* (Cambridge: Cambridge University Press, 1969), pp. 1-14.

[11]J. R. R. Tolkien, letter to Milton Waldman, in *The Letters of J. R. R. Tolkien*, ed. Humphrey Carpenter (London: Allen & Unwin, 1981), letter 131.

[12]*The Return of the King*, bk. 5, chap. 9.

[13]Tolkien, Letter to Milton Waldman.

[14]J. K. Rowling, "The Man with Two Faces," chap. 17 in *Harry Potter and the Philosopher's Stone* [*Sorcerer's Stone*, U.S.] (London: Bloomsbury, 1997).

[15]J. R. R. Tolkien, "On Fairy Stories," in *Tree and Leaf: Including the Poem "Mythopoeia"* (London: HarperCollins, 1992), p. 20.

[16]Tolkien quotes from E. A. Wallis Budge, *An Egyptian Reading Book for Beginners* (1896; repr., Mineola, NY: Dover, 1993), p. xxi.

[17]This concept of idolatry is also central to the thought of Owen Barfield, member of the Inklings and close friend of C. S. Lewis, in, for example, his *Saving the Appearances: A Study in Idolatry* (New York: Harcourt, Brace & World, 1965).

[18]C. S. Lewis, *The Allegory of Love* (Oxford: Oxford University Press, 1958), p. 44.

[19]It is also a dominant image in Lewis's fiction, such as in The Chronicles of Narnia, The Cosmic Trilogy, *The Great Divorce* and his short story "Light" (argued by Charlie Starr to be a later version of "The Man Born Blind").

[20]Verlyn Flieger, *Splintered Light: Logos and Language in Tolkien's World*

(Grand Rapids: Eerdmans, 1983), p. 49.

[21]J. R. R. Tolkien, *The Lord of the Rings*, "The Third Age" in appendix B.

Chapter 5: Right and Wrong as a Clue to Meaning

[1]C. S. Lewis, letter to Sister Penelope, July 9 (or August), 1939, in *Collected Letters of C. S. Lewis,* ed. Walter Hooper, vol. 2, *Books, Broadcasts and War 1931–1949* (London: HarperCollins, 2004), p. 262.

[2]J. Gibb, ed., *Light on C. S. Lewis* (London: Geoffrey Bles, 1965), p. 34.

[3]Charles Williams, quoted in Walter Hooper, *C. S. Lewis: A Companion and Guide* (London: HarperCollins, 1996), p. 302.

[4]*The Listener*, all issues, has been digitized and has limited availability in archive at http://gale.cengage.co.uk/product-highlights/history/the-listener-historical-archive.aspx.

[5]Justin Phillips, *C. S. Lewis at the BBC* (London: HarperCollins, 2002), p. 71.

[6]James Welch, quoted in ibid., p. 78.

[7]C. S. Lewis, quoted in ibid., p. 82.

[8]The BBC talks were first published as slim hardbacks—*Broadcast Talks* (1942), *Christian Behaviour: A Further Series of Broadcast Talks* (1943) and *Beyond Personality: The Christian Idea of God* (1944)—before being combined and revised in *Mere Christianity.*

[9]Carolyn Keefe, *C. S. Lewis: Speaker and Teacher* (Grand Rapids: Zondervan, 1971), pp. 87-88.

[10]J. B. S. Haldane, *Possible Worlds: And Other Essays* (1928; repr., London: Chatto & Windus, 1932), p. 209. Lewis had presented his argument in chapter three of *Miracles* (1947), which he revised after his debate with Anscombe, clarifying concepts that he recognized he had used unclearly or inaccurately. The revision appeared in the paperback edition of 1960.

Chapter 6: Exploring What Is Wrong with the World

[1]See P. D. James's "Who Killed the Golden Age of Crime?" *Spectator*, December 14, 2013, www.spectator.co.uk/features/9097312/a-nice-gentle-murder.

[2]Dorothy L. Sayers, preface to *The Devil to Pay* (London: Victor Gollancz, 1939), p. 7.

[3]Ibid., p. 10.

[4]Ibid., p. 11.

[5]Ibid.

[6]See Diana Pavlac Glyer, *The Company They Keep: C. S. Lewis and J. R. R. Tolkien as Writers in Community* (Kent, OH: Kent State University Press, 2007), pp. 58-59, and 73 n. 12. I discuss the pledge in more detail in chap. 7, "Space, Time, and the 'New Hobbit,'" of my *J. R. R. Tolkien and C. S. Lewis: The Gift of Friendship* (Mahwah, NJ: Paulist Press, 2003).

[7]C. S. Lewis, letter to Sister Penelope, July 9 (or August), 1939, in *Collected Letters of C. S. Lewis*, ed. Walter Hooper, vol. 2, *Books, Broadcasts and War 1931–1949* (London: HarperCollins, 2004), p. 262.

[8]Chad Walsh, *The Literary Legacy of C. S. Lewis* (London: Sheldon Press, 1979), p. 250. He refers also to Lewis's Narnian stories. These, together with the Ransom trilogy, demonstrate the achievement of Lewis's "visionary mind."

[9]Marjorie Nicolson, *Voyages to the Moon* (New York: Macmillan, 1948), p. 254.

[10]*Perelandra* is the first of two remarkable retellings of ancient myth (in his literary rather than popular sense of *myth*, where imagination renders truth, however unfocused, and not simply a fiction). This retells the account of Adam and Eve in the fictional context of the unspoiled world of the planet Venus. The other is *Till We Have Faces*, written nearly twenty years later, which retells the classical myth of Cupid and Psyche (see chap. 10). Both Lewis regarded as being among his very best work.

[11]One morning, soon after his arrival on Perelandra, Ransom awakes on a floating island and thought at first he was dreaming. "He opened his eyes and saw a strange heraldically coloured tree loaded with yellow fruits and silver leaves. Round the base of the indigo stem was coiled a small dragon covered with scales of red gold. He recognized the garden of Hesperides at once" (C. S. Lewis, *Perelandra* [London: Bodley Head, 1943], p. 49).

[12]Lewis makes it clear that the Green Lady is human, rather than only an alien rational species like the Hrossa or Sorns, for example, on Malacandra. This is despite the fact that there are no genetic connections between humans on Earth and humans on Perelandra. In one instance, Lewis describes the Green Lady and Ransom walking together as "the human pair" (*Perelandra*, chap. six). Her humanity and that of her husband, the King, is essential to the plot.

[13]Lewis, *Perelandra*, pp. 37-38.

[14]G. C. D. Howley, "Evil," in *The Illustrated Bible Dictionary* (Leicester, UK: Inter-Varsity Press, 1980), 1:487.

[15]C. S. Lewis, *Voyage to Venus* (London: Pan Books, 1953), p. 62.

[16]Ibid., p. 61.

[17]Ibid., pp. 107-8.

[18]See Lewis's essay "Why I Am Not a Pacifist," in *C. S. Lewis: Essay Collection and Other Short Pieces*, ed. Lesley Walmsley (London: HarperCollins, 2000), pp. 281-93.

[19]George Orwell, "The Scientists Take Over," *Manchester Evening News*, August 16, 1945, www.lewisiana.nl/orwell.

[20]See T. A. Shippey, *J. R. R. Tolkien: Author of the Century* (London: Harper Collins, 2000), e.g., pp. 119-21.

Chapter 7: Progress and Regress in the Journey of Life

[1]Valentine Cunningham, *British Writers of the Thirties* (Oxford: Oxford University Press, 1989), p. 226.

[2]C. S. Lewis, *The Pilgrim's Regress*, 3rd ed. (London: Geoffrey Bles, 1950), p. 22.

[3]Ibid., pp. 63-64.

[4]Ibid., p. 61.

[5]Lewis makes it clear that Mother Kirk stands for Christianity, not the Church, in his third edition (see ibid., p. 14, particularly). This third edition contains an explanatory preface to his allegory and annotations throughout.

[6]C. S. Lewis, "Preface to the Third Edition," *The Pilgrim's Regress* (London: Geoffrey Bles, 1950), p. 13.

[7]J. I. Packer, "Living Truth for a Dying World: The Message of C. S. Lewis," in *The J. I. Packer Collection*, ed. Alister E. McGrath (Downers Grove, IL: InterVarsity Press, 2000), p. 274.

[8]Lewis, "Preface to the Third Edition," pp. 11-12.

[9]C. S. Lewis, letter to Belle Allen, January 19, 1953, in *Collected Letters of C. S. Lewis*, ed. Walter Hooper, vol. 3, *Narnia, Cambridge, and Joy 1950–1963* (London: HarperCollins, 2007), p. 282.

Chapter 8: The Divide Between Good and Bad

[1]Jesus pictured this divide as a great gulf or chasm between heaven and hell in his vivid parable of the rich man and Lazarus in Luke 16:19-31.

[2]C. S. Lewis, *The Great Divorce* (London: Geoffrey Bles, 1946), pp. 66-67.

[3]C. S. Lewis, *Mere Christianity* (1952; repr., London: Collins Fontana, 1961), pp. 170-71. Lewis said he borrowed the parable from George MacDonald.

Chapter 9: The Power of Change

[1] Narnia's middle world between dangers to north and south echoes the *mappa mundi* of *The Pilgrim's Regress* (see chap. 7).

[2] Tolkien was not so averse to The Chronicles of Narnia to stop him recommending and lending them to his granddaughter Joanna Tolkien when she was young.

[3] C. S. Lewis, *Miracles*, rev. ed. (New York: Collins Fontana, 1960), p. 112.

[4] Similarly, in *The Great Divorce* the bus carrying ghostly visitors from hell passes through a tiny crack in the solid earth of heaven's borderlands.

[5] C. S. Lewis, letter to Anne Jenkins, March 5, 1961, in *Collected Letters of C. S. Lewis,* ed. Walter Hooper, vol. 3, *Narnia, Cambridge, and Joy 1950–1963* (London: HarperCollins, 2007), pp. 1244-45. The letter is held in the manuscript collections at Queen's University, Belfast, where Lewis's mother, then Flora Hamilton, studied.

[6] C. S. Lewis, *Prince Caspian*, Chronicles of Narnia (New York: Macmillan, 1951), p. 150.

Chapter 10: Pain and Love

[1] C. S. Lewis, *The Four Loves* (London: Geoffrey Bles, 1960), pp. 138-39.

[2] C. S. Lewis, *The Four Loves* (New York: Harcourt, Brace, 1960), p. 19.

[3] Ibid., p. 13.

[4] Ibid., p. 87.

[5] Charles A. Hutter, "Till We Have Faces: A Myth Retold," in *The C. S. Lewis Readers' Encyclopedia*, ed. Jeffrey D. Schultz and John G. West Jr. (Grand Rapids: Zondervan, 1998), p. 405.

[6] Chad Walsh, *The Literary Legacy of C. S. Lewis* (London: Sheldon Press, 1979), p. 245.

[7] C. S. Lewis, *On Stories: And Others Essays on Literature* (Orlando: Mariner Books, 2002), p. 47.

[8] "Recognition," in *Encyclopedia of Fantasy*, ed. John Clute and John Grant, 1997, http://sf-encyclopedia.uk/fe.php?nm=recognition, p. 109.

[9] Douglas A. Gresham, introduction to C. S. Lewis, *A Grief Observed* (San Francisco: HarperSanFrancisco, 2002).

[10] C. S. Lewis, *A Grief Observed* (New York: Bantam, 1976), p. 3.

[11] J. Gibb, ed., *Light on C. S. Lewis* (London: Geoffrey Bles, 1965), p. 63.

[12] W. H. Lewis, "Memoir of C. S. Lewis," in *Letters of C. S. Lewis*, ed. W. H. Lewis (London: Geoffrey Bles, 1966), p. 23.

[13]Lewis, *A Grief Observed* (San Francisco: HarperSanFrancisco, 2002), p. 6.

[14]Lewis, *A Grief Observed* (New York: Bantam, 1976), p. 1.

[15]Ibid., pp. 55-56.

[16]Denise Imwold, quoted in *501 Must-Read Books*, ed. Joanna Smith (London: Bounty Books, 2006), p. 208.

[17]Lewis, *A Grief Observed* (New York: Bantam, 1976), p. 31.

[18]Ibid., p. 51.

[19]C. S. Lewis, letter to Vera Gebbert, August 5, 1960, in *Collected Letters of C. S. Lewis*, ed. Walter Hooper, vol. 3, *Narnia, Cambridge, and Joy 1950–1963* (London: HarperCollins, 2007), p. 1177. Some think that Lewis is less clear in distinguishing an intermediate state between death and resurrection, and the state of the resurrected body, in his book *Letters to Malcolm: Chiefly on Prayer.*

[20]Lewis, *A Grief Observed* (New York: Bantam, 1976), p. 66.

[21]Lewis, letter to Sister Madeleva, October 3, 1963, in *Collected Letters*, 3:1460.

[22]Lewis, *Collected Letters*, 3:516-17.

[23]Don W. King, *C. S. Lewis, Poet: The Legacy of His Poetic Impulse* (Kent, OH: Kent State University Press, 2001), p. 244.

[24]C. S. Lewis, *A Grief Observed* (London: Faber & Faber, 1966), p. 29.

Chapter 11: Release from Hell's Snares

[1]C. S. Lewis, "The Weight of Glory," in *Screwtape Proposes a Toast and Other Pieces* (London: Collins Fontana, 1965), p. 109.

[2]C. S. Lewis, *Surprised by Joy* (London: Geoffrey Bles, 1955), chap. 15.

[3]C. S. Lewis, *The Screwtape Letters*, rev. ed. (New York: Macmillan, 1961), letter 3, para. 2; letter 6, para. 3; letter 14, para. 5.

[4]C. S. Lewis, *The Problem of Pain* (London: Geoffrey Bles, 1940), pp. 68-69.

[5]Ibid., p. 140.

[6]C. S. Lewis, *God in the Dock* (Grand Rapids: Eerdmans, 1970), p. 195.

[7]C. S. Lewis, *Mere Christianity* (New York: Macmillan, 1954), p. 128.

[8]Ibid., p. 38.

[9]C. S. Lewis, "The Weight of Glory," p. 94.

[10]Christopher Lasch, *The Culture of Narcissism: American Life in an Age of Diminishing Expectations*, rev. ed. (London: W. W. Norton, 1991), p. 210.

[11]This, of course, is not to deny that the self we present to others, the public

self or persona, is gradually created and constantly modified by us. (But even then, in a nonmaterialist view, it is the real self which creates our public face, presumably based on how we inwardly articulate the reality we experience.)

[12]See chapter 2, "Divine Omnipotence," in Lewis's *The Problem of Pain* (London: Geoffrey Bles, 1940).

[13]C. S. Lewis, *Till We Have Faces* (New York: Time Life Books, 1966), p. 268.

[14]C. S. Lewis, *The Problem of Pain* (New York: Macmillan, 1940), p. 91.

[15]Lewis, *Problem of Pain*, p. 79.

[16]C. S. Lewis, *An Experiment in Criticism* (Cambridge: Cambridge University Press, 1965), p. 138.

[17]Ibid., pp. 140-41.

[18]C. S. Lewis, "The Inner Ring," in *The Weight of Glory and Other Addresses* (1941; repr., Grand Rapids: Eerdmans, 1965), pp. 56-57.

[19]Ibid.

[20]This section draws upon my article "The Way of Friendship," *Christian History* 88 (2005), www.christianitytoday.com/ch/2005/issue88/10.37.html.

[21]C. S. Lewis, *Surprised by Joy* (New York: Harcourt Brace Jovanovich, 1955), p. 199.

[22]C. S. Lewis, *That Hideous Strength* (1945; repr., New York: Scribner, 1996), p. 111.

[23]See my *J. R. R. Tolkien and C. S. Lewis: The Gift of Friendship* (Mahwah, NJ: Paulist Press, 2003).

[24]C. S. Lewis, *The Four Loves* (London: Collins Fontana, 1963), pp. 58-59, 68.

[25]Ibid., p. 83.

[26]For more on this, see my *C. S. Lewis: A Biography of Friendship* (Oxford: Lion, 2013).

Chapter 12: The Way of Goodness and the Far Country

[1]C. S. Lewis, *The Problem of Pain* (London: Geoffrey Bles, 1940), p. 133.

[2]Ibid., p. 133.

[3]In *Surprised by Joy* Lewis tells us that in his stage of idealism before actually becoming a theist, he learned a valuable lesson: "What I learned from the Idealists (and still most strongly hold [as a Christian]) is this maxim: it is more important that Heaven should exist than that any of us should reach it" (chap. 13).

[4]C. S. Lewis, *Surprised by Joy*, in C. S. Lewis, *Selected Books* (London:

HarperCollins, 1999), pp. 1347-48.

[5]C. S. Lewis, "The Weight of Glory," in *The Weight of Glory and Other Addresses* (1941; repr., Grand Rapids: Eerdmans, 1965), p. 11.

[6]C. S. Lewis, *Prayer: Letters to Malcolm*, in Lewis, *Selected Books*, p. 617.

[7]Lewis, *The Problem of Pain*, pp. 133-34.

[8]C. S. Lewis, *The Lion, the Witch and the Wardrobe*, chap. 7. As there are numerous editions, I shall only cite chapters for Narnia books.

[9]C. S. Lewis, *The Voyage of the Dawn Treader*, chap. 16.

[10]Corbin Scott Carnell, *Bright Shadow of Reality: C. S. Lewis and the Feeling Intellect* (Grand Rapids: Eerdmans, 1974), p. 161.

[11]C. S. Lewis, *The Magician's Nephew*, chap. 8.

[12]J. R .R. Tolkien, *The Monsters and the Critics and Other Essays*, ed. Christopher Tolkien (London: George Allen & Unwin, 1983), pp. 153-55.

[13]J. R. R. Tolkien, *The Two Towers*, chap. 8.

[14]J. R. R. Tolkien, *The Fellowship of the Ring* (New York: Houghton Mifflin Harcourt, 2012), pp. 189-90.

[15]J. R. R. Tolkien, *The Letters of J. R. R. Tolkien*, ed. Humphrey Carpenter (London: George Allen & Unwin, 1981), letter 131.

[16]J. R. R. Tolkien, *Sauron Defeated: The History of Middle-earth*, ed. Christopher Tolkien (New York: Houghton Mifflin Harcourt, 1992), 9:296-99.

[17]*Imram* was published in *Time & Tide*, December 3, 1955. Available with difficulty for many years, it was published in ibid.

[18]For a full account see Donald S. Johnson, *Phantom Islands of the Atlantic* (London: Souvenir Press, 1997).

[19]Warren H. Lewis, *Brothers and Friends: The Diaries of Major Warren Hamilton Lewis* (San Francisco: Harper & Row, 1982), p. 194.

[20]Johnson, *Phantom Islands*, p. 169.

[21]Wayne Martindale, *Beyond the Shadowlands: C. S. Lewis on Heaven and Hell* (Wheaton, IL: Crossway, 2005).

[22]C. S. Lewis, *Last Battle*, chap. 15.

[23]Ibid.

[24]On this important contrast, see Colin Duriez, "Myth, Fact, and Incarnation," in *Myth and Magic: Art According to the Inklings*, ed. E. Segura and T. Honegger (Zollikofen, Switzerland: Walking Tree, 2007), pp. 71-98, and Colin Duriez, "The Theology of Fantasy in Lewis and Tolkien," *Themelios* 23 (1998): 35-51.

Appendix 1: War in Heaven

[1]In a modern version of Book of Common Prayer, in the section for baptism, this is rendered, "Fight valiantly . . . against sin, the world and the devil." See "Believe and Trust: Holy Communion with Baptism," *Church of England*, accessed November 3, 2014, www.churchofengland .org/prayer-worship/worship/texts/newpatterns/sampleservicescontents /npw7.aspx.

[2]See *The Legend of Sigurd and Gudrún*, trans. J. R. R. Tolkien, ed. Christopher Tolkien (New York: Houghton Mifflin Harcourt, 2009). As a child Tolkien read a retelling of the story in Andrew Lang's *Red Fairy Book*.

[3]C. S. Lewis, "De Descriptione Temporum," in C. S. Lewis, *Selected Literary Essays*, ed. Walter Hooper (Cambridge: Cambridge University Press, 1969), pp. 1-14.

[4]See C. S. Lewis, "Satan," in *A Preface to Paradise Lost* (London: Oxford University Press, 1942), chap. 13.

[5]Lewis, "Dedication to Charles Williams," in *Preface to Paradise Lost*, p. v.

[6]Charles Williams, "An Introduction to Milton's Poems," in *The English Poems of John Milton*, World's Classics Edition (London: Oxford University Press, 1940), pp. vii-xx.

[7]C. S. Lewis, *A Preface to Paradise Lost* (Oxford: Oxford University Press, 1961), p. 95.

[8]Ibid., p. 96.

[9]*Paradise Lost*, bk. 5, line 662.

[10]Lewis, *Preface to Paradise Lost*, p. 96.

[11]Ibid., p. 97.

[12]*Genesis A*, trans. Lawrence Mason, Yale Studies in English 48 (New York: Henry Holt, 1915).

[13]Genesis does not say that the earth belongs to humankind, with the implication that we are free to make conquest of it and to do with it whatever we like. The earth is the Lord's, and we find our home here as God's children.

[14]Augustine, *Sermons* 261; trans. and ed. Henry Bettenson, *The Later Christian Fathers: A Selection From the Writings of the Fathers from St. Cyril of Jerusalem to St. Leo the Great* (Oxford: Oxford University Press, 1977), p. 222. There is more on St. Augustine's view of evil, as we saw, in chap. 4.

[15]A key analysis is Jacques Ellul's *The Technological Society* (New York: Alfred A. Knopf, 1964).

[16]Martin Heidegger, "The Question Concerning Technology," 1977, para. 7, http://simondon.ocular-witness.com/wp-content/uploads/2008/05/question_concerning_technology.pdf.

[17]C. S. Lewis, *The Screwtape Letters*, Letter VII.

Appendix 2: The Spirit of the Age

[1]For a full treatment of subjectivism, see Jerry Root, *C. S. Lewis and a Problem of Evil* (Eugene, OR: Pickwick, 2009).

[2]C. S. Lewis, "The Poison of Subjectivism," in *Christian Reflections* (London: Geoffrey Bles, 1967), p. 73.

[3]Ibid.

[4]C. S. Lewis, *Letters to an American Lady* (Grand Rapids: Eerdmans, 1967).

[5]C. S. Lewis, *The Abolition of Man* (1945; repr., New York: Macmillan, 1955), p. 25.

[6]Clyde S. Kilby, *The Christian World of C. S. Lewis* (Appleford, UK: Marcham Manor Press, 1965), p. 101.

[7]Lewis, *Abolition of Man*, pp. 56-57.

[8]C. S. Lewis, "The Empty Universe," in *Present Concerns*, ed. Walter Hooper (London: CollinsFontana, 1986), pp. 81-82, 83. This was Lewis's preface to D. E. Harding's *Hierarchy of Heaven and Earth* (London: Faber & Faber, 1952).

[9]It is instructive how often the theme does occur, however. In *Miracles*, for instance, Lewis argues against a subjective view of truth, implicit, he shows, in a materialistic, or naturalistic, view of the world.

[10]Lewis, *Abolition of Man*, pp. 87-89.

Index